The widely reprinted Spanish classic, now in English...

The Silence of Mary

Translated
from the original Spanish edition

The Silence of Mary

by
Ignacio Larrañaga, O.F.M., Cap.

Translated from the Spanish by
V. Gaudet, O.M.I.

Pauline
BOOKS & MEDIA

Boston

Library of Congress Cataloging-in-Publication Data

Larrañaga, Ignacio.
  [Silencio de María. English]
  The silence of Mary / by Ignacio Larrañaga ; translated from the
Spanish by V. Gaudet.
        p.   cm.
  Translation of: El silencio de María.
  ISBN 0-8198-6911-2
  1. Mary, Blessed Virgin, Saint.   2. Silence—Religious aspects—
Christianity. I. Title.
BT602.L2913 1991
232.91—dc2O   91-34526
                                                          CIP

Original Title: *El Silencio de María*

Copyright © 1979, Cefepal, Santiago de Chile

Translated from the Spanish by Rev. V. Gaudet, O.M.I.

English edition copyright © 1991, Daughters of St. Paul

Printed and published in the U.S.A. by Pauline Books & Media,
50 St. Paul's Avenue, Boston, MA 02130.

http://www.pauline.org   E-mail: PBM_EDIT@INTERRAMP.COM

Pauline Books & Media is the publishing house of the Daughters of
St. Paul, an international congregation of women religious serving
the Church with the communications media.

2 3 4 5 6 7 8 9   04 03 02 01 00 99 98 97

At daybreak, she was still among us;
like a flag abandoned in the desert.
—Gibran

In memory of my mother, María Salomé,
with love,
Fr. Ignacio Larrañaga, O.F.M., Cap.

Contents

Part Three

Silence

PART FOUR

The Mother

PART ONE
BACK TO THE ORIGINS

All my springs are in you.
—cf. Psalm 87

CHAPTER 1

The Sealed Fountain

Who first told the story of the infancy of Jesus? How did we come to know these events so distant in the past, whose archives could be found only in the memory of Mary?

To answer these questions we need to go back. And to go back we must go up, up against the current of a river which carries dramas and surprises, until we come to the remote well that was the heart of Mary.

The Gospel recalls for us two occasions (cf. Lk 2:19; 2:51) in which Mary carefully preserved distant words and events from the past. And she meditated on them attentively. What does this mean? It means that Mary sought the deep, hidden sense of those events and words, and applied them to the new situations she encountered in her life.

In this way the memories remained most vividly in her mind, like stars that never fade. Hence, whatever roads we choose to follow in order to see the face of Mary and hear the palpitations of her heart, these roads must necessarily lead us far away to the fountain from which these realities spring to life: the intimacy of Mary.

"Our Beloved Physician" (cf. Col 4:14)

> Luke is a writer of great talent and delicate soul, an engaging and ever transparent personality.[1]

Luke is a man deeply sensitive to the motivations which animated the person and life of Mary, as, for example, her humility, patience, meekness. Whenever Luke meets with a trace of mercy, he is deeply moved. Immediately he notes it in his Gospel.

Our medical evangelist detects and appreciates the soul of woman and her importance in life; Luke does this better than any other evangelist. Through the pages of his lengthy and packed Gospel there is a parade of various women: one receiving mercy, others offering hospitality, a group expressing sympathy and solidarity with Jesus as he walked the pilgrimage toward his death. And from the midst of them all Mary emerges with the unmistakable air of a servant and lady.

Luke's singular personality is one of delicacy and sensitivity. It is significant that Paul speaks of him with an emotional overtone as "our beloved physician." Thus our evangelist seems to possess a temperamental affinity with the personality of Mary.

In conclusion we are encountering the ideal narrator, one who was able to enter into perfect harmony with our Lady, able to identify not only the facts of her life but also her vital impulses, and what is more, able to transmit all of this with fidelity.

Investigating and Transmitting

> Since many have undertaken to compile a narrative of the events that have been fulfilled among us, just as those who were eyewitnesses from the begin-

ning and ministers of the word have handed them down to us, I too have decided, after investigating everything accurately anew, to write it down in an orderly sequence for you, most excellent Theophilus, so that you may realize the certainty of the teachings you have received.

—Luke 1:1-5

Following the literary custom of his day, Luke dedicates his work to the "excellent Theophilus." We do not know who this illustrious addressee was. However, through the introductory words we can conclude that Luke is dealing with a high-ranking person who had already received the Word and embraced the faith. Nevertheless Luke does not address him as a "brother." Why? Because of some social distance? Because his work is destined for the larger public? Whatever the reason, this "Theophilus" disappears without any further trace of his existence.

Luke speaks here as a modern journalist who, to guarantee the credibility of his information, testifies that he was present at the "place of the events." In this way, as though to certify the objectivity of his work and the validity of Theophilus' faith, Luke prepares to give an account of the purpose, the content, the sources and the working method of his writing.

❖

First of all Luke asserts that many before him have undertaken this same task of investigation. They compiled documents and made collections of the actions and words of Jesus. Some of them even composed some form of a gospel.

This observation of "our beloved physician" is most interesting. It means that Luke, before beginning his task as a researcher, and while carrying it out, had in his possession collections of facts and sayings and perhaps even gospels authored or compiled by others. Some of these writings were lost, while others eventually came to be used by Luke himself. Among these writings would there not be recollections of Mary compiled by some disciple—memories of the distant days of the annunciation and of the infancy of Jesus?

At the outset, Luke makes a highly important statement: he asserts that he had investigated everything carefully (cf. Lk 1:13), all the events which make up the high point of salvation. In modern language we would say that Luke put into use the historical critical method. And thus he presents in his book a new arrangement, new details found in his diligent investigation, perhaps also a more rigorous verification of the facts, and all this in new literary garb.

"From the Beginning"

For our purpose, which is to know Mary, it is interesting to ponder and appreciate the fact that Luke, with his "careful investigation," returns to the remote circumstances of what happened "from the beginning."

Our historian, with the lamp of "historical criticism" in his hands, went back and shed light on a journey filled with surprise and suspense. He traveled through a complicated chain of events, until he reached the early days of our Lady. It is obvious that the historical critique of Luke would not be as rigorous and precise as that of modern scholars. Nonetheless, he carried out a serious investigation, attempting to arrive not only at the origin of the events but also at those earliest days.

From the words of the evangelist, the following idea

deserves emphasis: apparently Luke made use of manuscripts or reports transmitted by eyewitnesses, that is, by those who were at the very heart of the events and of the struggles. If that is so, then Mary is the only eyewitness for the events of Jesus' infancy. We can therefore conclude that the evangelist, whether through direct or indirect means nobody knows, arrived at that unique source of information: Mary.

On the other hand, we are invited to imagine situations which carry great weight: indeed the context of Luke manifests most clearly that the eyewitnesses became thereby "ministers of the Word." Could we then conclude that Mary also became an evangelist of these events about which she alone was knowledgeable? Did Luke want to indicate in a veiled or implicit way that the presence of Mary in the first Palestinian communities was not only one of animation but of dedication to an activity that was specifically missionary? In a word, among the multitudes of eyewitnesses who proclaimed the Word must we include Mary? The study of sources leads us to this very conclusion. (See Chapter Two, "Features for a Photograph.")

The First Years

After Pentecost, when the apostles spread over the earth to announce the "news" of the last hour, they bore in their souls the marks of some deep psychological scars, if you allow me this expression.

What had occurred? A chain of events that shook them deeply. On a day not long past, confounding everything that they "were hoping" for (Lk 24:21), successive events fell upon Jesus, master and leader. Like a whirlpool, these events engulfed him and carried him inexorably to his crucifixion and death. The apostles themselves only narrowly escaped the same fate.

As a consequence they were crushed, disoriented, hopeless and full of fears (cf. Lk 20:19).

A few days later came the resurrection, and the apostles experienced a most violent shock which carried them, like a hurricane, almost to paroxysm. They appeared overwhelmed, bewildered, as if they were robots who could not prove what they were seeing and hearing. They did not expect the crucifixion nor the resurrection, in spite of the fact that both events had been predicted to them. After a few weeks more, the Holy Spirit arrived and he explained it all. For the first time they began to understand the word of Jesus, his person and his central function in the history of salvation. At last everything became clear.

And from this moment, in going out to the world, the apostles bore two deep "wounds": the death of Jesus and his resurrection. These were the fundamental events, this was the paschal mystery. Scattered over the world, the apostles began to talk. They seemed to be obsessed. For them nothing was important apart from the events that *saved:* the humiliation and the exaltation of Jesus. Only this saved. For all the rest, who cared? In these first years the apostles could speak about nothing else.

❖

In this frame of mind, that which had no direct reference to the paschal mystery had no significance for the apostles nor any importance. This is why they left out details which are so pleasing to our modern taste: Where and when was Jesus born? What happened to him during those first years? Who were his parents? What were they like? What was the exact chronological order of events?

All these and similar preoccupations were for the evangelists useless curiosity. The biographical data had no importance, only the saving events did.

Thus, with this state of mind and hierarchy of values we can easily understand that the stories relating to the infancy of Jesus had no fundamental value in their eyes, at least during the first years. Nor did the events relating to the person of Mary have much importance.

The first years passed. Then, one day, these events began to cause interest and make the rounds in the Palestinian communities. How did this happen?

When the first communities under the inspiration of the Holy Spirit began to proclaim Jesus as *"Kyrios," the Lord,* they felt the need to complete the historical perspective of the Lord Jesus. They needed to know who this unique person was historically, where he was born, how he lived, what he taught.

Now, in this great realm of silence that surrounded Jesus, there was no eyewitness but Mary. And she became the evangelist of the events which were ignored by all others.

What About the Internal Criticism?

Nevertheless, these questions are still without answers. Who was the recipient of Mary's secrets? Who was the author of the first two chapters of Luke? Assuming that Luke was not the original source of these pages, where did these reports come from? And how did they fall into the hands of Luke?

Following the investigations of the great German exegete, Paul Gechter, we shall first state that Luke was not the author of these pages, but that he found them in his efforts as a researcher and inserted them into his Gospel.

In reality it is improbable if not impossible for Luke to have received this information directly from the lips of Mary. If he wrote his Gospel between the years 70 and 80 A.D., (a chronology highly uncertain, yet to date the most proximate), it is hard to imagine Mary would have lived that long. She would have been more than ninety years old. According to measurements of longevity in an underdeveloped country, it cannot be assumed that Mary would have lived so many years. Therefore we must discard the hypothesis that Luke received from the lips of Mary direct reports about the infancy of Jesus.

❖

Moreover, the internal critique of these two charming chapters also undermines the hypothesis of the authorship of Luke. The internal structure of these pages is entirely semitic, as also the general style with the cadence and rhythm of its expressions.

Luke was born in Antioch, a Greco-Roman city, more than a thousand kilometers, some 850 miles, from the biblical scenario. Besides, he was born a pagan, as is clearly deduced from the context of the fourth chapter of the letter to the Colossians.

In contrast, the person who wrote those first two chapters was entirely familiar with the semitic mentality and with the general Old Testament inspiration. It is difficult to imagine that a convert, one who had not been raised on biblical inspiration from the time of infancy, would be so knowledgeable of the text and context of the Old Testament, as the author of those two chapters appears to have been.

The medical evangelist came across these notes, then, and inserted them into his Gospel. The activity of Luke as regards these chapters, if ever there was such activity, must have been insignificant, like that of one who makes only minor changes.

> The legitimate conclusion is that Luke copied the Greek document as he found it, even though on occasion he may have adapted it to his own literary taste.

> The cultural background that is reflected in the minor details, the semitic formulation of dialogues, exclude all Lukan intervention of any importance.[2]

After a critical evaluation tremendously complicated and solid, Paul Gechter arrives at the same conclusion:

> The cultural framework which the narrative of the infancy presents to us excludes Luke, pagan by birth, as the composer of the first two chapters of his Gospel, just as he is undoubtedly excluded by the general structure, the language and the rhythm.

> The presence of this culture in Luke 1 and 2 can be explained only if one admits that Luke found the Jewish document with the narrative of the infancy and inserted it into his Gospel, practically without retouching it.[3]

Much later, Gechter reiterates the same conclusion based upon an impressive analysis, adding the following:

> The totally semitic nature of the general structure, cultural flavor and rhythm of the expressions demonstrates that the creative and transforming activity of Luke had to be very secondary.[4]

John, the "Son"

If Luke was not the confidant who received the information about Jesus' infancy nor its material author, through what means did these precious notes come into his hands?

According to the normal calculations of probability, the first person we think of is the apostle John who, above all, received and pondered the confidences of Mary. As we know, "from that hour," John received Mary "into his home" (Jn 19:27). This expression, so full of meaning, points to a limitless life of communion. Between Mary and John there would have been neither secrets nor reservations. John must have taken care of Mary in a singularly delicate manner, with great affection and veneration now that she was approaching the close of her life.

Between two people of such interior beauty there must have existed an inexpressible unity which was far beyond the affectionate relationship of a mother and son.

It seems to me that the first to have received the confidences of Mary was the "son John." However, in this book we shall see how Mary did not communicate to anyone the deep secrets of her heart, except perhaps to Elizabeth. But even in this case, we must not forget that when Mary reached Ain Karim, the Fundamental Secret was already in the heart of Elizabeth, surely given to her directly by God (cf. Lk 1:39ff.)

Nevertheless, internal critique indicates that John was neither the compiler nor the author of these notes. The style of John is unmistakable. John did preserve a few remembrances of the life of Jesus. On the basis of those remembrances, John continued meditating deeply on the transcendental mystery of Jesus all through his life. This theological reflection is expressed in his writings in the form of key words such as Life, Love, Light, Truth, Way.... The beloved disciple did not write two pages in which some of these key words do not appear.

In those Lukan chapters there is nothing which indicates the authorship of John.

Mary, a Missionary

If the authors were neither Luke nor John, who were they? What happened?

We have to turn back until we arrive at that closed and sealed chamber. The news could go from mouth to mouth as the waters of a stream flow from rock to rock. But how and when did Mary open that sealed spring?

In the Gospels, groups of women appear in the company of Jesus. The evangelist doctor indicates that, at a distance, looking on the agony of the crucified one, were "the women who had followed him from Galilee" (Lk 23:49). Were these the same women who served him with their means during the days of Galilee? (cf. Lk 8:2ff.)

John recalls that after Jesus had manifested his glory in Cana, his mother came down with him to Capernaum (cf. Jn 2:12). And the same John places Mary with other women at the foot of the cross (cf. Jn 19:25).

Later we shall see in what manner Mary belonged to this group of disciples, transforming herself into a "disciple" of Jesus, not so much as a human mother as in an attitude of faith.

Here then, behold Mary forming part of a group of women, even in Jesus' time, as in a school of formation. We do not know the degree of intimacy which existed between Mary and these women. But it is obvious that being enthusiastic followers of Jesus, they would seek to know from Mary the details of his infancy and ask about periods of his life which nobody knew of except her.

> Without doubt these women disciples of Jesus must have questioned Mary repeatedly about Jesus' infancy and youth.[5]

Time passed. Then came events which took everyone by surprise. The Comforter came. Under his inspiration the community confessed Jesus Christ and Lord. With these exalted events Mary could not hide the wonders that had been worked in those earlier days. This would be the precise hour for revealing the hidden stories.

How was it done? I cannot imagine Mary visiting the communities as a wandering preacher, announcing *kerygmatically*, like a trumpet, the untold story of Jesus. Well then, what did happen?

Paul Gechter, in his voluminous dossier of arguments, supposes and demonstrates, beginning with internal criticism, that there was a small and intimate circle of women who first received the confidences of Mary. Their remembrances were strictly maternal and were kept in this motherly and intimate atmosphere, so feminine.

> The stamp of motherhood is suspected not only from the subject that was treated, but also from the little interest shown in juridical questions.[6]

> All memories are colored by a maternal perspective.[7]

> The environment more suited to the transmission of the story of the infancy of Jesus was a feminine world. Children are the eternal attraction of women.[8]

❖

Researchers who study the real life context of the first communities point out a phenomenon which is quite moving. They say veneration for Mary blossomed almost from the first moments in the first communities. Harnack says: "The circle from which the narratives of the infancy proceeded felt a great veneration for Mary. They placed her on the highest level together with her Son."

From his investigation, Rudolf Bultmann also concludes that the first Christian communities felt "a special and well known devotion toward the Mother of the Lord."

❖

We must therefore conclude that there existed a group of women who gathered around Mary with great confidence and affection. This group felt a profound veneration for her, not only because, as Mother of the Lord her very being was venerable, but also because her composure was marked by a constant dignity, humility and peace.

One of these feminine circles was, then, the depository of her confidences and stories when our Lady became convinced that the end of her existence was near, and that there should be no more secrecy about her Son, who was now openly proclaimed Christ and Lord. Mary would speak in the first person, and these women would express the words of Mary in the third person, according to a simple grammatical convention. They would perhaps add some detail of little importance so as to enhance the central role of Mary.

These memories of Mary possibly fell into the hands of a disciple who possessed some notion of theology. He may have made some incidental alterations. And in this way, the manuscript, copied many times by hand, began to circulate among the Palestinian communities.

Luke, who had been researching among the eyewitnesses and among the first communities, came upon this authentic jewel, and inserted it into his Gospel.

> Consequently we must think primarily of a small feminine circle which manifested a great veneration toward Mary. Their interest in the infancy of

> Jesus put Mary under the obligation of narrating some episodes; this she did from the visual standpoint of a mother.
>
> This visual standpoint naturally was received and preserved by these women as an immutable deposit.
>
> Through these women the news filtered down to a disciple who made in them some alterations in line with the more rigorous theological thinking of the very first days.[9]

This means that the stories contained in the first two chapters of Luke were communicated directly by Mary. These stories, except for a few refinements of form, came from the lips of our Lady. This intimacy and proximity is why they preserve such a sense of immediacy. Moreover they are words which are in complete harmony with the personality, the conduct and the reactions of Mary.

As we will show throughout this book, Mary always occupies a second place in the narrative, precisely because these are words which came from her own lips. In these chapters we will encounter praise-filled descriptions of Zechariah, of Elizabeth, of Simeon and Anna. About herself almost nothing is said.

Humility and modesty permanently envelop the life of our Lady like an aura. Never is she the center of attention. Mary always proclaims and submits. She submits to the Other. Only God is important.

CHAPTER 2

Features for a Photograph

We have plunged into the deep but not very clear waters of the first communities. We return with many impressions and intuitions, and also some conclusions.

Along with these impressions I intend to try to sketch a few personal characteristics of Mary. These characteristics will be spelled out throughout this book.

Jesus was born according to the flesh, and his first days unfolded between persecutions and flights. It was Mary, his Mother, who cared for him and defended him. Jesus—the Church—was born according to the Spirit in the midst of a storm, and once again it was Mary who defended him, consoled him and strengthened him.

Nevertheless, we have the impression that this motherly role of Mary in the primitive Church was exercised in a manner which was as discreet as it was effective. The author of the Acts of the Apostles was either not aware of this, or did not give it any importance, or, at least, did not record it in his book. We have the impression that Mary acted silently, as usual, behind the scenes, and thus influenced the newborn Church.

The Mother

Who was she for the community? What did the community call her? It would not have been the name of Mary. That name was too common: Mary of Clopas, Mary of James, Mary of Magdala. A name was needed to better signify her personal identity. What would that name be?

The community lived constantly in the presence of the Lord Jesus and addressed praise and supplication to him. Now, how should a community which lives with Jesus and in Jesus identify and name that woman? The answer came of its own accord: she was the Mother of Jesus. Hence it was always in this way that the Gospel refers to her.

But in reality Mary was more than the Mother of Jesus. She was also the mother of John, and she was the mother of the disciples—including all those who found their identity in the name of Jesus. Was this not the role with which she was entrusted by the lips of the dying Redeemer? Thus she was simply *the Mother,* without any other qualification. One has the impression that from the very first moment Mary was identified and differentiated by this role and possibly by this precious name. This seems to be inferred from the name the four Gospels give Mary whenever she appears on the scene.

We shall see in another part of this book in what way Jesus, through a disconcerting and painful pedagogy, was leading Mary from a purely human motherhood to a motherhood in faith and in the Spirit. Mary had given birth to Jesus according to the flesh. Now that the birth of Jesus according to the Spirit at Pentecost was approaching, the Lord needed a Mother in the Spirit.

Thus Jesus was preparing Mary through a transforming revolution for a spiritual function. Because of this, Jesus often appears in the Gospel to discount purely human motherhood. Yet, at the coming of Pentecost, Mary was already prepared; she was already Mother according to the Spirit. She appears to be presiding and giving birth to the first small cell of the Twelve who would constitute the Body of the Church.

❖

According to what is said of her in the Gospels, Mary was never a passive nor an alienated woman. She questioned the proposition of the angel (cf. Lk 1:34). On her own she took the initiative and rapidly crossed the mountains of Judea to help Elizabeth in the last months of her pregnancy and first days after childbirth (cf. Lk 1:39). In the grotto at Bethlehem she and she alone took care of herself in the complicated and difficult hours of childbirth (cf. Lk 2:7). For such a task, how can a man be useful?

When the child was lost, the Mother did not remain idle, wasting her time. She quickly joined the first caravan, went up to Jerusalem—a distance of close to a hundred miles—and searched all around for Jesus for three days (cf. Lk 2:46). At the wedding of Cana, while everyone was enjoying themselves, she was the only one keeping watch. When she realized that wine was missing, she took the initiative again, and without disturbing anyone, she delicately sized up the situation. And she found the solution.

At another moment, when she heard rumors that Jesus' health was not good, she took the initiative and presented herself at the house in Capernaum to bring him back, or at least to take care of him (cf. Mk 3:21). On Calvary, when all was consummated and nothing else could be done, Mary kept watch in silence (cf. Jn 19:25).

It is easy to imagine what a woman of such personality would accomplish during the delicate circumstances of the newly-born Church.

I can easily imagine the words that she must have addressed to the group of disciples when they left for distant lands to proclaim the Name of Jesus. I can imagine the consoling and encouraging words she proffered to Peter and John after their arrest and flogging. I can even imagine how she must have treated their wounds with oil and vinegar, the way the best of nurses would have done.

Knowing how she acted during the days of the Gospel, I can infer that Mary, as she had been on Calvary, was there with the "devout men [who] buried Stephen" (Acts 8:2).

I can imagine how she, who was so service-minded, instead of standing by idly, found herself among the seven men "filled with faith and the Holy Spirit," serving the tables of the Greek women (cf. Acts 6:5). I have not a single doubt that the Mother was the first woman "deaconess" in the original sense of the word.

She who had been such an excellent recipient and guardian of the news (cf. Lk 2:19; 2:51)—I can imagine how she transmitted the reports about the spread of the Word of God in Judea and among the Gentiles (cf. Acts 8:7), and how, with those reports she strengthened the hope of the Church.

This woman who once instructed, "Do whatever he tells you" (Jn 2:5), I can imagine now visiting the communities with the same words on her lips: "Do whatever he commands you to do." If the Church did remain constantly in prayer, might it not have been because of the insistence and example of the Mother?

This was a unique sight. The members of these communities lived in close unity. They held everything in common. One saw them always cheerful. Never would they use possessive terms such as "mine," "yours." They hastened daily and with zeal to the Temple and enjoyed the sympathy of all. In a word, they were of one mind and one heart. All of this made a tremendous impression on the town. Never had such a thing been seen.

Who brought about this remarkable sight of such harmony? Would it not have been the Mother, that Lady so full of peace and composure? How often must she have visited the communities repeating: "Remember how he told you so often: 'Love one another'! Remember that this was his last will. Do what he commanded you: 'Love one another!'"

❖

There in Bethlehem, in Egypt, in Nazareth, Jesus was nothing without his Mother. She taught him how to eat, how to walk, how to speak. Mary did the very same thing for the newborn Church. She was always behind the scenes. The disciples knew where Mary would be: in John's house. Would it not have been the Mother who encouraged and maintained in prayer those committed to Jesus? (cf. Acts 1:14)

Would it not have been the Mother who advised the apostles to fill in the void left by Judas, so as to fulfill the details of the original plan of Jesus? (cf. Acts 1:15ff.)

To whom would John go to be consoled after his difficult encounters? Did he not live with the Mother? Who encouraged John to go daily to the Temple and to private homes to proclaim the great news of the Lord Jesus? (cf. Acts 5:42) Behind such a man we sense the touch of one who inspires courage.

The day Stephen was stoned to death, a furious persecution erupted against the Church in Jerusalem. The followers of Jesus dispersed into Samaria and Syria. The apostles, nevertheless, decided to remain in the theocratic capital city (cf. Acts 8:1ff.). On that day, where did the apostles gather to find consolation and strength? Would it not have been at John's home, close to the Mother of them all?

In those first years, John and Peter always appear together. If Mary lived in John's house and there continued to inspire and guide him, wouldn't she do the same for Peter? Wouldn't both Peter and John, who venerated Mary so highly, hold their reunions in John's house, together with Mary? Wouldn't she have been the counselor, the consoler, the animator—in a word, the heart of that Church which was born among persecutions? Would not the house of John have been the meeting place in moments of trials and in moments of important decision-making?

If we note the personality of Mary, and if we judge from her reactions and general behavior in the days of the Gospel, then according to the normal weight of probabilities, we can conclude that all these questions must be answered in the affirmative.

The Bible was written according to certain cultural forms. Many of its pages were written in a patriarchal society, in an atmosphere of prejudice against women. It is a known fact that in the Greco-Roman world as in the world of the Bible, women were marginalized. In that context it was bad form for a writer to highlight the extraordinary actions of a woman. If it had not been for this prejudice, how many marvelous things would the book of Acts have spoken, wonders silently worked by the Mother!

❖

Then, between the years 90-95 A.D., when he was more than eighty years old, the "son" John recorded a very distant but very moving event.

At the culminating moment, from the cross, Someone entrusted him with a mission having the urgent character of a last wish: "John, take good care of my mother. Do it in memory of me." He wanted to tell him much more; this much at least did he say. Since that time many years had elapsed. Now all John remembered was that he had taken her into his home. Nothing more. But how much life is expressed in these few words! How meaningful they are!

How was this life? What was the height and depth of communion between these two exceptional beings?

We already know John. His soul is made transparent in his writings as in a mirror, ardent as fire, soft as the breeze. John was an affectionate man, of that type of persons whom solitude depresses and who blossoms like a flower when in company. We know Mary: silent as peace, attentive as a lighthouse, open as a mother.

It seems to me that in this world there has never been a relationship like this between persons of such beauty. How could this be? Who was caring for whom? The son for the Mother, or the Mother for the son? There are words in the dictionary which, because they are overused, lose their charm. These words, in the relationship between Mary and John, recover their original freshness: love, delicacy, care, veneration.... All these and much more were intertwined in the intimacy in which these two privileged persons lived. It was something inexpressible.

When these two spoke of Jesus, both called upon their personal memories. That shared meditation, in which these two ardent and penetrating souls began to navigate the deep waters of the transcendent mystery of the Lord Jesus Christ, must have been beyond description. Could the Gospel of John not have been the fruit of the theological reflection between Mary and John?

With what care did John look after the Mother during her declining years, when her spirit was soaring into high altitudes! With what suspense, grief and near-adoration did John attend her ineffable passage of death and close her eyes!

Surely John was the first to experience that which we call "devotion to Mary": filial love, admiration, availability, faith....

The Holy Spirit

There's something about Mary! Wherever she is present, there is also an energetic presence of the Holy Spirit. This has happened since the day of the Incarnation. On that day—I do not know how to explain it—the "Person" of the Holy Spirit took total possession of Mary's world. From that day on, the presence of Mary has unleashed a spectacular radiance of the Holy Spirit.

When Elizabeth heard Mary's greeting, she was immediately "filled with the holy Spirit" (Lk 1:41). When Mary went into the Temple with the Child in her arms, waiting her turn to be purified, the Holy Spirit fell upon the elderly Simeon making him speak prophetic and disturbing words.

On the morning of Pentecost, when the Holy Spirit with fire and earthquake rushed violently over the group of the chosen ones, wasn't Mary, the Mother, there? (cf. Acts 1:14) I do not know what relationship came into existence back then, but there seems to have been a profound and mysterious kinship between these two "persons."

The book of Acts was given the name "Gospel of the Holy Spirit" with good reason. There is hardly any chapter in Acts in which the Holy Spirit is not mentioned three or four times. This is where the first steps of the Church are described. Wouldn't it be true to say that this newborn Church, presided over by the invisible presence of the Holy Spirit, was also presided over by the silent presence of the Mother?

A mysterious, profound relationship exists between both persons. It seems that the presence of Mary always coincides with the presence of the Holy Spirit. This mystery will become clearer when we speak about motherhood.

If the apostles received all sorts of gifts on that great awakening of Pentecost, we can imagine the fullness she would have received who, on another occasion, was blessed with that personal and fruitful presence of the Holy Spirit.

Moreover, the boldness and self-assurance of the disciples can be explained by another reason, one I would call "psychological." Mary, the Mother, was behind the scenes. Everyone knew that she was there in John's house and under his care. In this home John was the new son. But in this home all felt they were likewise sons.

Truly, the most appropriate title given to Mary is *Mother of the Church!*

❖

Through these reflections we have come to understand:

—Mary left an indelible impression on the soul of the early Church.

—From the very first moments, the Church felt a lively kinship with the Mother and surrounded her with love and veneration.

—Cult and devotion to Mary go back to the first heartbeats of the newborn Church.

> An exegesis which sees, hears and understands the beginnings, testifies to the veneration and the joy which were then and have always been increasingly felt in her regard.[10]

PART TWO
THE PILGRIMAGE

She "advanced in her pilgrimage of faith."
—LG 58

Remain silent before the Lord, and trust in him.
—cf. Psalm 37

CHAPTER 3

An Eternal Journeying

To believe is to surrender. To surrender is to walk before the face of the Lord. Abraham is an eternal traveler toward a supreme Fatherland, and this Fatherland is God himself. To believe is always to set out.

Before we begin to contemplate Mary's faith, I wish to reflect extensively not on the nature of faith but on the ways it can be lived. In a word, faith as a fellowship with God.

In this world nothing is easier than to manipulate concepts of God and thus build fantastic castles in the air. There is nothing more difficult than arriving at the encounter with that same God who is always beyond words and concepts. For this we must cross the forest of confusion, the sea of dispersion and the unfathomable darkness of the night. In this way we can arrive at the clarity of the Mystery.

The Mystery

God is as untouchable as a shadow and at the same time as solid as a rock. The Father is eminently Mystery and this mystery neither allows itself to be grasped nor analyzed: it must simply be accepted in silence.

God is not at the tip of our fingers, as the hand of a friend which we can lovingly grasp. We cannot control God like we can handle a book, a pen or a watch. We cannot tell him: "Come to me tonight; tomorrow you can leave." We cannot manipulate him.

God is essentially disconcerting because he is essentially gratuitous. The first act of faith is to accept the gratuity of God. Faith is a continuous getting up and a continuous setting out to search for a Someone whose hand we can never grasp. The second act of faith consists in accepting in peace this profound sense of frustration.[1]

❖

However, if the Father is an inaccessible Mystery, he is also a fascinating one. If you approach him only a little, he illumines and warms you, but if you approach him more closely, he inflames. The Bible is a multitude of people aflame.

The Bible says that we cannot look him in the face, that God cannot be contained by the human mind, as long as we sojourn in this world. Neither can he be possessed in a vital way. This will only be possible once we have gone beyond the frontiers of death. If someone were to "see his face," while still a pligrim on earth, that person would die (cf. Ex 33:19-23).

In other words, the Lord cannot be subject to the normal proceedings of our human knowledge. All the expressions we use to understand him and who he is are only comparatives, analogies, approximations. For example, when we say that God is a father, we should add immediately that he is not exactly a father, that he is more than a father—better yet, that he is something other than a father.

Another example: we know in our own human language what the word *person* means. When we wish to ex-plain who God is and what God is like, we use this con-cept applying it to God: we say that God is a person. But God is not exactly a person, although in a sense he is. In a word, God cannot be imprisoned in concepts, let alone in human words. All the words we use to refer to him can only be used in a negative way: *"im*-mense, *in*-finite, *in*-visible, *in*-effable, *in*-comparable." This is what is meant in the Bible when it says that no one can see the face of God (cf. Ex 33:23).

Thus God is always beyond our words and concepts. He is absolutely "The Other," or absolutely absolute. Speaking precisely, God cannot be the object of understanding. Rather, he must be the object of faith. This means that one does not understand God; one accepts him. The one who accepts God on his knees, "understands" him better.

❖

We know that the Father is always with us, but it will never be possible for us to touch him nor will anyone be able to see his eyes. These are comparisons to express, once again, that the Father is absolutely different from our perceptions, conceptions, ideas and expressions...the word "God" is one thing, and *God himself* is quite another. Words will never be able to contain the immensity, the richness and the depth of the total mystery of our beloved Father.

This is why in the Bible, God is the one who cannot be "named." There are three questions in the biblical context which contain an identical sense: Who are you? What are you? What is your name? On the mountain

Moses asks God his *name.* God answers with the word *"being."* "Moses said to God: '...if they ask me, "What is his name?" what am I to tell them?' God replied, 'I am who am.' Then he added, 'This is what you shall tell the Israelites: I AM sent me to you'" (Ex 3:13-14). God responds evasively. He is "the One without a name," the Ineffable. In this way the Bible beautifully expresses the transcendence of God. Elsewhere when God is asked his name his response is significant: "Manoah (the father of Samson) said to the angel of the Lord: 'What is your name...?' The angel of the Lord answered: 'Why do you ask my name? It is mysterious'" (cf. Jgs 13:17-18). Thus not only is the name of God inexpressible and mysterious, but so are the names of his servants and of everything directly connected with him.

❖

Our life as believers is a journey among shadows in search of the Father's mystery. In this world we can find obscure traces of him but never his face.

The brilliant stars in the deep of the night can evoke the mystery of the Father, but the Father himself is far beyond the stars, and much closer. Music, flowers, birds can evoke God, but *God himself* is far beyond all such beauty.

No one has lived in such familiarity with all these sister-creatures as Francis of Assisi. For him all creatures were a theophany or transparency of God. But when Francis wanted to meet with *God himself,* he retired to dark, solitary caverns.

Traces

Hence God is above and beyond our ways of thinking, our mental processes, intellectual representations, inductions and deductions. This is why our faith is a pilgrimage—because we need to keep searching among deep shadows for the face of the Father.

At times we see the traces of some feet that have passed over the sand and we say, "A human being has passed by here." We can even add: "He was an adult, he was a child. There are the footprints." In this same way we are discovering the mystery of God on the earth. At other times we come to know him through deductions and we say: "This has no other possible explanation than to admit a creative intelligence." Our journey in the realm of faith is thus made possible through the path of analogies, evocations and deductions.

Could a person blind from birth guess at some point the color of a flame of fire? Colors have never entered his mind. This is why he cannot identify, recognize and distinguish colors. Colors transcend him. Could the retina ever capture just the tiniest spark of God's majesty? He cannot enter into our games, into the circle of our ideas. He is above. He transcends us. Our Father is an immortal and living God over whom neither night nor death nor deception will ever fall. Never will he be attained by sound, light, fragrance or any of our human devices.

❖

God cannot be conquered by the weapons of our intelligence: to conquer God means to allow ourselves to be conquered by him. God can only be received; he can only be welcomed. In a word, the Lord God is fundamentally the object of faith. We cannot "catch" God; it is impossible to master him intellectually. We are pilgrims. We continually set off, and we never arrive.

Because of this, for the people of the Bible, God is not a mental pastime. He is one who produces tension, generates drama. A person of the Bible is continually wrestling with God. What a paradox it is that to triumph in this singular combat, we must let ourselves be attacked and conquered, as Jacob did that night on the bank of the river (cf. Gen 32:23-33).

Due to this, the Lord always calls his people to this combat in the solitude of the mountains, the deserts, the caverns: to Sinai, to the river Jabbok, to Mount Carmel, to Mount Olivet, to Mount Alvernia, or to the cave of Manresa....

Dissatisfaction and Nostalgia

There was One who came from the Father's house, and he told us that the Father is like a jewel which projects a light different from our light. Such is its splendor that it is worth selling everything we own so as to possess this treasure. Before our astonished eyes Jesus, the One who was sent, has presented the Father as a luminous sunset, a resplendent sunrise, thus enkindling in our hearts the fire of an infinite nostalgia for him.

He came to tell us that the Father is so much greater, more marvelous, and more magnificent than anything we can think of, dream about, conceive or imagine. St. Paul puts it this way: "Eye has not seen, ear has not heard, nor can the human heart imagine what God has prepared for those who love him" (cf. 1 Cor 2:9). Whoever is devoured by this nostalgia is one on the journey.

In addition, even before the earthly coming of Jesus, God had created us in his own image. He has sown in our innermost being a sign of his own self. He made us like a well of infinite depth which cannot be filled with innumerable natural things, but only with the Infinite. Our faculties and senses can be satisfied, but *we* always remain dissatisfied. Yet even one who is dissatisfied is on the journey.

❖

We are strangers among all other creatures. We feel like eternal exiles, consumed by an infinite nostalgia for him whom we have never seen; we yearn for a father-land we have never lived in. A strange nostalgia indeed!

While the stone, the oak, or the eagle feel fulfilled and do not aspire to more, we are the only creatures who can feel dissatisfied, frustrated. Beneath our satisfactions blazes the fire of a profound dissatisfaction. At times, it is half-extinct under gray ashes; at other times it is transformed into a devouring flame. This dissatisfaction is the other side of our nostalgia for God, and it turns us into travelers searching for the face of the Father. This dissatisfaction is therefore, for us, at once a curse and a blessing.

What is man? He is like a living flame, spiraling toward the stars, always willing to lift up his arms to cry out, "O Father!" A child who cries continually, "I'm hungry! I'm thirsty!" A dreamer of limitless lands beyond our horizons, of stars which light up beyond our nights. A pilgrim of the Absolute, as he was called by the French author, Leon Bloy.

A Desert

To believe is therefore an eternal trudging along dark and almost always deserted ways, because the Father always hides within deep shadows. Faith is precisely this: to go on a pilgrimage, to ascend, to weep, to doubt, to hope, to fall and to get up again, and always to walk like nomads who do not know where they will sleep at night, or what they will eat tomorrow. Like Abraham, Israel, Elijah, and Mary.

The crossing of Israel from Egypt to the land of Canaan was a symbol of such faith. The desert which can be crossed today in a few hours meant for Israel forty years of sand, thirst, hunger, sun, agony and death.

Israel left Egypt and was lost in the desert among mountains of sand and rock; there were days in which hope seemed dead and the horizons closed up. Then God appeared as the sweetest of shadows in the form of a cloud which shielded them from the burning rays of the sun. At times, also, in our own pilgrimage, God is like this: when his face is transformed into presence, there is nowhere in the world a sweetness greater than God.

At other times, the night was dark and heavy for Israel: they were afraid and they could see nothing. Then God would present himself in the form of a torch made of stars; the night would be as bright as midday, and the desert would be transformed into an oasis. But the pilgrimage, for the most part, was a desert.

❖

The same happens in our own pilgrimage. We sometimes have the feeling that everything is too much for us, but suddenly spring blossoms and the day is bright. Then, by late afternoon it darkens, the sky is covered by thick clouds, and at night the firmament is void of stars.

Thus does our life go on: today we feel secure and happy, because the smile of God shines over us and temptations cannot overcome us. Tomorrow, the Father's sun hides itself, we feel as weak as a reed, and anything upsets us. Envy devours us. We wish to die. We feel like unfaithful, unhappy children and we cry out: "Father, come quickly, take me by the hand!"

In this life of faith, for pilgrims who truly seek the face of God, there is nothing so unbearable as the absence of the Father, even though, through the eyes of faith which sees what is essential, the Father is always present. There is no sweetness more inebriating than that of sensing the presence of the Father as he begins to show himself from behind the clouds.

The Crisis

In Kadesh-Barnea, Israel was trapped between sand and silence. They realized that the desert could be their tomb. All around them loomed the deep, threatening shadows of discouragement, fear and the craving to turn back. The silence of God fell over them. Terrified, the faith pilgrims began to cry out: "Moses, where is God?" "Is the LORD in our midst or not?" (Ex 17:7).

Even the disciples, on hearing Jesus speak about the Eucharist, thought that they were hearing the words of a mad person. "Who can eat human flesh?" They said, "This is asking too much. This saying is hard. The Master has lost his mind. Let's go." And they abandoned him (cf. Jn 6:66).

When Abraham, Gideon and other warriors for God felt surrounded by the thickest darkness, silence and void, they desperately sought for a solid support, because they felt they were groping among shadows, sailing over threatening waters. They pleaded with God for help, for a "sign" so that they would not succumb (cf. Gen 15:8; Jgs 6:17; 1 Sm 10:1-7).

This is how it is in our lives. We often feel like children lost in darkness: discouragement and fear invade our souls. We feel abandoned, alone, and we begin to doubt that behind this silence the Father is really there, together with us. The crisis follows, and we ask ourselves if the words have any substance. To live by faith is a debilitating pilgrimage like the crossing of the sea during a storm.

Awakening

Then the day of our death will arrive. On that day the pilgrimage will end, liberation will be ours and we shall contemplate the resplendent face of the Father for all eternity.

Faith also will die, as an old lamp whose light we no longer need. The same will happen with hope. As a fragile yet powerful ship that has brought us through the waves, nights and storms, to the promised harbor, it will be abandoned on the shore. Finally we shall land on solid ground, entering always more deeply into the infinite regions of God.

Only love, life, the eternal abode of God, will remain. Now all that is left is to live eternally submerged, permeated and penetrated by the splendor of a Presence which will calm and satiate all desires. We shall repeat eternally: "O Father, infinitely loving and eternally loved!" These words will never grow old.

CHAPTER 4

Blessed Are You, Because You Believed

The life of Mary was no tourist adventure. On a tourist jaunt we know which restaurant we will eat in today, which hotel we will sleep in tonight, which museum we will visit tomorrow. Everything is foreseen; there is no room for surprise.

It was not so with the life of Mary. She was also a wanderer. She traveled the same roads we travel, and in her wanderings she encountered all that is characteristic of a pilgrimage: jolts, confusion, perplexities, surprises, fears, fatigue. Above all she was filled with questions: "What is this? Is this true? And now what do we do? I see nothing. Everything is dark."

Among the Shadows

The child's father and mother were amazed at what was said about him.

—*Luke 2:33*

But they did not understand what he said to them.

—*Luke 2:50*

From the days of Moses there was an ordinance that every first-born male—human or animal—was to be a special property of the Lord. The first-born animal was offered in sacrifice; the first-born son was "ransomed" by his parents, according to a price stipulated by the law. According to the same levitical decrees which dated from the days of the desert, the woman who had given birth remained "impure" for a set period, and she had to present herself in the Temple so as to be declared "pure" by the priest who was taking his turn of service.

So Mary was in the Temple of Jerusalem, with the Child in her arms, near the door of Nicanor at the eastern wing of the vestibule for women. Stirred by the Holy Spirit a venerable old man came into the midst of the group. His life had been like a flame, sustained by hope. That life was just about to be extinguished.

The venerable old man took the Child from the arms of his Mother and, addressing himself to the pilgrims and to the faithful, spoke to them some strange words: "Adorers of Yahweh, this Child whom you see in my arms is the Awaited One of Israel. He is the light that will glow over all nations. He will be a banner of contradiction. All will take sides about him, some in favor and others against. There shall be death and resurrection, ruin and restoration. And now, I can close my eyes; I can die in peace, for all my hopes have been fulfilled" (cf. Lk 2:28ff.).

What was Mary's reaction on hearing these words? She remained silent, "amazed" by all that had been said (cf. Lk 2:33). Everything seemed so strange. She was amazed? A proof that she did not know something, that she did not understand everything about the mystery of Jesus. Astonishment is a psychological reaction of surprise at something unknown and unexpected.

❖

Previously there had been a similar episode. It was a night of glory. Some shepherds had been taking their turn keeping watch over their sheep. Surprisingly, a divine splendor enveloped them like a light. They saw and heard things they could never have imagined. They were told that the Awaited One had arrived. This was the reason for so much joy and song. They were invited to pay him a visit of courtesy; and the signs to help them identify the Awaited-One-Already-Come were these: a manger and swaddling clothes (cf. Lk 2:8-16).

The shepherds ran swiftly and found Mary, Joseph and the Child. They told everyone what they had seen that night.

The evangelist adds: "All who heard it were amazed by what had been told them by the shepherds" (Lk 2:18). Who were "all who heard it," those who were so amazed? To know this we have only to go back two previous verses: "They...found Mary and Joseph, and the infant" (Lk 2:16). These, then, were the ones who were amazed.

❖

They were days of agitation and shock...Mary and Joseph searched for their Child, for several days. At last they found him in the Temple. The Mother burst out, emotionally: "What have you done to us?" This was a sort of release after the nervous energy that had built up during these stress-filled days.

The answer of the Child was dry, cutting and distant. "Why are you so worried about me? A great distance separates me from you. My Father is my only occupation and concern." It was a real declaration of independence: his sole and total commitment was to the Father.

What did Mary do? She remained paralyzed, understanding nothing (cf. Lk 2:50), sailing in a sea of darkness, wondering what these words, and above all, this attitude meant.

❖

These three scenes indicate clearly that the actions and words of Jesus, that is, his transcendent nature, was not entirely understood by his Mother, or at least not immediately assimilated.

The information about Mary's amazement (cf. Lk 2:18; 2:33) and ignorance (cf. Lk 2:50) could not have been known except from the very lips of Mary. The community, which venerated her so much, would not have offered on its own account information that would diminish the merit and veneration of the Mother. This means that such information must have been historically objective and that it could only come from the lips of Mary.

Parenthetically, the scene remains extremely moving: the Mother, in the midst of the community, explaining to a group of disciples, naturally and objectively, that she did not understand these words, that other words remained most surprising to her. The Mother was most touchingly humble. Mary was fundamentally humility itself.

It is not correct to say that Mary was flooded by a powerful infusion of knowledge, nor that, because of permanent and exceptional graces, she was freed from all obscurities, that all veils were lifted, that all horizons were opened to her, and that from her childhood she knew everything concerning the history of salvation, and all that referred to the person and destiny of Jesus.

This is contrary to the text and context of the Gospels.

Here is the reason so many Christians feel a kind of uneasiness about Mary. Some have idealized her so much they have made a myth of her. They have placed her out of our reach, so far out of our human ways that many have come to feel, without knowing why, deeply personal reservations about that mystical woman excessively idealized.

The life of Mary had nothing to do with tourism. Just like us, she gradually discovered the mystery of Jesus Christ with the attitude typical of the "poor of Yahweh": surrender, humble searching, a trusting availability. The Mother too was a pilgrim traveling empty roads and dark valleys, gradually searching for the face of God and the will of the Father—just like us.

❖

In the Gospel of Mark we find a strange episode full of mystery. The context of this narration seems to indicate that Mary did not comprehend with sufficient clarity the personality and destiny of Jesus, at least during those early times of evangelization. What happened?

From the first three chapters of Mark we could conclude that the initial performance of Jesus among the cities of Galilee was sensational. It produced lively discussions and a consequent division about Jesus among the Jews and even among his own relatives (cf. Jn 10:19).

There is no doubt that Jesus was considered a strange character, even by his own relatives, so much so that because of his powerful miracles and speeches they thought he had lost his mind (cf. Mk 3:21). The fact is that one day these relatives decided to take hold of him and bring him home. In the general context of chapter 3 we might deduce that at the head of that group of relatives was Mary herself (cf. Mk 3:20-22; 3:31-35).

From the psychological nature of this attitude we can conclude that at the time Mary did not have an exact knowledge of the nature of Jesus. In reality what was it all about? Did Mary share in some measure the disappointment her relatives felt over the powerful manifestation of Jesus' ministry? Was Mary among those who wanted to take him home or did she simply want to take care of him because "he did not have even the time to eat"? (cf. Mk 3:20)

Once more we arrive at the same conclusion: Mary traveled our paths of faith. She was also searching among shadows for the true face of Jesus.

❖

At the wedding of Cana we observe that Mary had taken definite steps in the knowledge of the profound mystery of Jesus. In her first reaction she acted on a merely human level. She acted as a mother who enjoys some sort of ascendency over her son; she felt in communion with him and proceeded as one who felt certain of being granted a great favor.

> Mary believes that she lives in communion with her Son, but she finds herself alone.
>
> Later, seeing that she is not in that communion, she enters into a new relationship with him, in the communion of faith: "Do whatever he tells you" (Jn 2:5). It does not matter what she says, what matters is what he says, even though she does not know as yet the decision of Jesus.[2]

At this moment all was now clear in the mind of Mary. It did not matter that her motherly glory had been tarnished. She now knew that for Jesus all is possible, a concept the Bible reserves exclusively to God.

> If Mary was not able to be granted a favor from Jesus in virtue of her maternal right, she obtained it in virtue of a superior right, that of her communion with him through faith.
>
> Her faith is authentic. It is neither a pretension nor a demand but a trust in him who can do all he wishes to do, when his hour has come, because it must be so.[3]

Significantly, John adds that after this episode Mary went down with Jesus to Capernaum (cf. Jn 2:12). What does this mean? That Mary stepped down from being a mother in order to become a disciple? Does it mean that the Mother, on seeing this prodigy, was freed from all doubts, that she overcame this mixture of light and darkness, and that she definitively entered into total brightness?

Between Light and Darkness

What is there between light and darkness? The penumbra, which is nothing but a mixture of lights and shadows. According to the Gospel texts, this was Mary's life: voyage on a sea of lights and shadows.

On the day of the annunciation, if we note the words that were then spoken, Mary had a complete knowledge of the One who would blossom in her silent womb: "He will be great and will be called Son of the Most High...and of his kingdom there will be no end" (Lk 1:32-33).

Surely the splendid visitation of God on that day brought an extraordinary infusion of light and knowledge. Above all it is certain that the personal and fruitful infusion of the Holy Spirit was accompanied by an abundance of gifts, particularly those of wisdom and knowledge. Because of the penetrating light of the Holy Spirit on that day, Mary saw everything most clearly.

In contrast to this, through the texts just analyzed, we see that Mary, later on, did not understand some things, and marveled at others. Well then, if on the day of the annunciation Mary understood completely the reality of Jesus, and later, it seems, did not understand this same reality, what happened in between? Does there exist here some contradiction? Was the evangelist who edited these texts misinformed?

❖

In my opinion this confused and contradictory background is full of human grandeur, and from this obscurity Mary emerges more brilliant than ever. She was not a demi-goddess, some strange phenomenon somewhere between a goddess and a woman. She was a creature as we are, an exceptional creature of course, but her being exceptional did not mean that she was not a creature and that she did not travel over the same paths we travel with their misfortunes and crossroads.

We need to put Mary into our own human experience. What happens to us could have happened to her, excepting always her highest fidelity to the Lord.

What happens with us? Let us think, for example, about persons consecrated to God through priesthood or religious life. One far off day, in the flower of their youth, they experienced the irresistible attraction of Jesus Christ. At that time the manifestation was like a blue midday sky: it was God who called, and he called them to a most sublime mission. This was so clear that they embarked with Christ on a most fascinating adventure.

Many years passed. How many of these consecrated persons feel confused today, think that God never called them, that consecrated life has no meaning? Why does something that was once like a bright sword now seem like a rusted piece of iron? We must look at this objectively: this is the way we are.

❖

They married. He said that there was no brighter star than she in all the heavens. She said that not even with Diogenes' lamp would she be able to find a person like him. Everyone said that they were made for one another. For a few years they were happy. Then routine filtered into their lives like a cursed shadow. Today their lives have given way to a sort of lethargy. Both think that they should have married someone else. How is it that what one day was so bright is now dark? We all have to arrive at the same conclusion: we are made this way. We are not geometrical. The human being is not made according to straight lines.

This is the way we are: a few securities and a mountain of insecurities. In the morning we see clearly; at noonday we begin to doubt and at night everything is dark. One year we espouse one cause, the next, disappointed, we lose interest in that same cause.

❖

Because of this human tendency, winding and wavering, we may explain the fact that Mary saw clearly at one particular moment of her life and apparently did not see so clearly at another.

Would it be disrespectful toward Mary to think that she also felt the weight of the silence of God? Would it be improper to think that Mary was first the victim of deception, then of confusion and finally of doubt at a particular period of her life?

On the day of the annunciation, because of the solemn tone of that revelation, it seems that Mary was promised a journey resplendent with unending prodigy. But in the end, when the time came for her to give birth, she felt alone and abandoned. What is more, later she had to flee like a lowly political fugitive, and live under foreign skies. And during thirty interminable years there was nothing new, only monotony and silence.

What was she to rely on? On that which seemed to be promised on the day of the annunciation, or on the actual cold, hard reality? Would perplexity never perturb the serenity of her soul? What happens to us? Why should the same not happen to her?

"Mary kept all these things, reflecting on them...." (Lk 2:19)

What did Mary do during these moments of trial? She tells us herself: she held on to the ancient words so that she could now keep her balance.

These words were lamps. Mary kept them perpetually lit: she guarded them diligently and meditated on them in her heart (cf. Lk 2:19; 2:50). They were not dead leaves, but living memories. When new events were enigmatic and disconcerting, the bright lamps of ancient memories brought light to the dark perplexities of reality.

Thus Mary was advancing from ancient lights and present shadows toward total brightness. The various evangelical texts and their general context indicate clearly how Mary arrived at a gradual "comprehension" of the transcendent mystery of Jesus: she realized it by means of an unshakable adherence to the will of God which manifested itself through these new events.

❖

The same happens with us. Many persons have had in the past gratuitous visitations from God: they experienced his living presence, they received infused graces and extraordinary gifts. These moments have remained imprinted, like wounds, in their hearts. These were intoxicating moments.

Years pass. God is silent. These people are assaulted by dissipation and temptation. Monotony creeps in. The silence of God continues obstinately. These persons must take hold, almost desperately, of the memory of these wonderful experiences so as not to give in to despair.

The grandeur of Mary does not consist in the fact that she was never assaulted by confusion. It rests rather on the fact that when she did not understand something she did not react with anguish, impatience, irritation, anxiety or fright.

For example, Mary did not confront the twelve-year-old Child: "My son, I don't understand you. What happened? Please, tell me—quickly—what you mean by your attitude?" Mary did not say to Simeon: "Venerable old man, what do you mean when you speak about a sword? Why should this Child be a sign of contradiction?"

Instead, Mary takes the attitude of the "Poor of Yahweh": full of peace, patience and gentleness, she takes hold of the words, she enters within herself and, remaining recollected, reflects: "What did these words mean? What is the will of God in all of this?" Mary is like those flowers which, at the disappearance of the sun, turn inward. Thus she retreats within herself and, full of peace, she strives to identify herself with the disconcerting will of God, accepting the mystery of life.

❖

Unfortunately, we are similar to other creatures. Sorrowful circumstances surround us and we coil like implacable serpents. Everything resembles a blind fatality. Successive misfortunes have befallen us so surprisingly and with such brutality. Treason lurks in the shadows, and—who would have thought it possible? In our own home! At times, we are simply fed up with life, we may even wish to die.

What do we gain by rebelling against the inevitable? In such moments we are called to imitate Mary, to keep quiet and remain in peace. We know so little, but the Father knows all. If we can do anything to change the chain of events, let's do it. But why should we try to fight those things that we cannot change?

Mary tells us: "My children, come after me. Do what I did. Follow the same routes of faith that I have traveled and you will belong to the people of the Beatitudes. Happy are they who, in the midst of the darkness of night, believe in the splendor of the light!"

CHAPTER 5

Mary's Interior Life

To Surrender

To believe is to trust. To believe is to let go. To believe, above all, is to adhere, to surrender. In a word, to believe is to love. What is an intellectual syllogism worth if it does not even touch our life? It would then be like a musical score without a melody.

To believe is "to walk in the presence of God" (cf. Gen 17:1). Faith is at the same time an act and an attitude which grasps, involves and penetrates the whole of the human person: one's trust, faithfulness, intellectual assent and emotional adhesion. It lays open the entire history of a person: judgments, attitudes, general conduct and vital inspiration.

All this is fully realized in Abraham, the father and model of our faith. Abraham received an order: "Go forth from your land" (cf. Gen 12:1) and a promise: "I will make of you a great nation" (cf. Gen 12:2). Abraham believed. What did it mean for him to believe? It meant presenting the Lord with a blank check, to open an infinite and unconditional credit account, to trust against common sense, to hope against hope, to surrender blindly and without calculation, to break away from the status quo and, at his seventy-five years, to "put himself on the road" (cf. Gen 12:4) in the direction of an unknown world, "not knowing where he was to go" (Heb 11:8). This is what it means to believe: unconditional surrender.

Biblical faith is this: adherence to God himself. Faith does not principally refer to dogmas and truths about God. It is surrendering to his will. It is not primarily an intellectual process, a passage from premises to conclusions, a setting up of logical combinations, toying with a few concepts or mental presuppositions. It is, principally, a vital attitude.

Concretely it involves an existential adhesion to the person of God and to his will. When this interior adhesion to the Mystery of God exists, truths and dogmas are accepted naturally and do not present intellectual conflicts.

People of Faith

In the eleventh chapter of the Letter to the Hebrews, there is a descriptive analysis—in a certain sense, a psychoanalysis—of the vital nature of faith. It is one of the most impressive chapters of the New Testament: it resembles a gallery of immortal figures who parade before our astonished eyes. They are outstanding figures, sculpted by their adult faith: indestructible persons who possess a deep interior life which amazes and awes, persons capable of facing superhuman situations without ever allowing themselves to be separated from their God.

Through an "obstinate refrain" each verse in this chapter reminds us that such greatness is due to the individual's unconditional adhesion to a living and true God: "by faith," "in faith," "through faith." These expressions are continually repeated.

❖

The patriarchs appear sleeping in tents on the sand. Because of their faith they live wandering in a burning and hostile desert. They must always live in foreign lands where the inhabitants look on them with suspicious eyes (cf. Heb 11:8-13).

By faith others faced wild beasts, strangled lions, silenced the violence of devouring flames, and, I do not know how, succeeded in fleeing when the sword of the enemy was almost upon them. By faith they recovered strength in their weakness, and a handful of men, armed with an adult faith, turned back foreign invaders (cf. Heb 11:33-35).

Because of their faith, and in order not to betray their God, they peacefully accepted, without resistance, a violent death. Through faith, some endured in silence all kinds of injuries, others suffered forty stripes minus one without complaining. In faith they preferred the chains of prison to the freedom of the street. Not to be separated from their God, they did not even protest to being stoned.

In faith they ended their lives, some being "sawed in two," others "put to death at sword's point" (Heb 11:37). In order not to be unfaithful to their God they lived as wandering fugitives, climbing mountains, traveling through deserts, clothed in skins of sheep and goats—donning deceptive disguises so as to disorient their persecutors. They hid in grottoes and caverns, persecuted, starved, oppressed and tortured (cf. Heb 11:35-39).

All of this unforgettable drama was due to their faith—a faith that was not only an intellectual exposition or syllogism. They did these things so as not to be withdrawn from their living and true God. Their faith was an adhesion, full of love, for their God. Neither death, nor life, claims St. Paul, nor authorities, nor forces of oppression, nor visible or invisible enemies, nor heights nor depths, nor anyone in this universe can separate me from the love of Jesus Christ my Lord (cf. Rom 8:38-40).

A Declaration

In my opinion, these are the most precious words in Scripture: "Behold, I am the handmaid of the Lord. May it be done to me according to your word" (Lk 1:38). This declaration is also the key to Mary's heart and to perceiving her most intimate sentiments.

We know little about Mary, but we do know enough. It would suffice to apply the spirit and scope of this declaration to all the moments of Mary's life to find out what her reactions were in every circumstance.

The Enchanting Woman

Nazareth was an insignificant hamlet in northern Palestine, with a spring at the center of the town, surrounded by relatively fertile countryside jutting out into the valley of Esdraelon.

This is where Mary lived. According to calculations of the exegete, Paul Gechter, if we base ourselves on the customs of Palestine at that time, Mary must have been about thirteen years old at the time of the annunciation (Paul Gechter, *op. cit.* pp. 139-143). We cannot compare our girls of thirteen with the girls at the same age then. The aging curve differs notably according to climate, era, customs, and the coefficient of growth and longevity. It suffices to know that at that time the law considered twelve-year-old girls marriageable, and generally at that age they were promised in marriage. In any case, Mary was a very young girl.

In spite of being so young, the sublime and solemn words addressed to her by the angel on the part of God indicate that Mary possessed an interior maturity and emotional stability much superior and disproportionate to her age.

In fact it is significant that in his salutation the angel omits the proper name of Mary. The grammatical phrase "full of grace" is used as a proper name. Grammatically it is a perfect participle in its passive form, which we could translate: "Good day, *full of grace!*" This might be expressed today with the words, "enchanting woman," meaning God finds in Mary a most special delight or empathy.

We are then contemplating a young girl who has been the object of a divine predilection. From the first moments of her existence, before her birth, she was preserved from the hereditary sin which she ordinarily would have contracted and, simultaneously, like a garden carefully cultivated by the Lord God, she was irrigated with the most outstanding gifts, graces and charisms.

Because of this she is told that the "Lord is with her," a biblical expression that indicates an extraordinary assistance on the part of God. Nevertheless this does not mean that such special treatment transforms her into a heavenly princess, beyond our human experience. We should never lose sight of the fact that Mary was a creature like us, though treated in a special way for a most special destiny.

The Angel Came to Her

At this point, the one writing this, as well as the one who reads it, must adopt a difficult but necessary attitude, that of creating within ourselves a contemplative mood; we must hold our breath, enter into a state of suspense and approach, with infinite reverence, the interior life of Mary.

The scene of the annunciation was pulsating with profound intimacy. To understand this and what happened then, we must immerse ourselves in that interior mood and capture, more with the heart than with the mind, the vital context and secret invisible emotions of Mary. What did she feel? How did she see herself at this moment?

How did the annunciation come about? Did it happen in her house? Perhaps in the field? On the mountain? At the spring? Was Mary alone? Was it in the form of a vision? Did the angel take human form? Was it an unmistakable interior locution? The evangelist says, "And [the angel] coming to her..." (Lk 1:28). Must his "coming" be understood in a literal and spatial sense? For example, as someone who comes to the door, knocks and then enters into the house?

Could it be understood in a less literal and more spiritual sense? For example, let us suppose that Mary was in a state of deep intimacy with the Lord. She is overwhelmed by the embracing presence of the Father. Words have disappeared, communication between the servant and the Lord occurs in profound silence. Suddenly, this silence is interrupted. Into this intimacy between the two—an intimacy which ever remains an intensely private experience—someone "enters." Could the annunciation be explained in this way?

What we know with absolute certainty is that the normal life of the country girl was interrupted in a surprising manner by an extraordinary visitation of her Lord God.

> At the apparition and announcement of the angel, Mary felt troubled.
>
> In addition she, the one "full of grace," experienced the proximity of God as an awesome and disconcerting force.[4]

Two propositions are made to her, one as astonishing as the other. Mary did not expect this, far from it. She was living normally and humbly, abandoned into the hands of her Lord, as the sentinel waits for the dawn. Not only did she not expect this but she was left completely confused by it all.

The interpretation that Mary made of the double prodigy announced to her, according to what she confided to Elizabeth, was this: she, Mary, considered herself least among the women of the earth (cf. Lk 1:48). Anything great she did have was all without any merit of hers, but came from the Lord's gratuity and predilection. The wisdom of God chose precisely the most insignificant creature among all the women of the earth, to manifest and prove that God alone is the Magnificent One. He chose someone who was lacking in personal gifts and charisms, so that it would be clear to the world that the "great things" (Lk 1:49) of salvation are not the result of personal qualities but of the grace of God.

This was her interpretation. We are in the presence of an intelligent and humble girl who was inspired by the Spirit of Wisdom.

Two Propositions

First, Mary was informed that she would be Mother of the Messiah. This had been the golden dream of every woman in Israel, particularly from the days of Samuel. Between the salutation of the angel and this fantastic

proposition, the young girl was left "troubled," confused, like one who does not feel worthy of so much; she
was overcome by a sensation of deep emotion and bewil-
derment.

But Mary felt much more at odds with the second
proposition: this messianic motherhood would be
wrought without any human participation, in a miraculous manner. It would entirely transcend the biological
process and would produce an original and direct creation from the hands of the Almighty, for whom all is
possible (cf. Lk 1:37).

Before such an apparition and these most extraordinary propositions, one wonders: how could a young girl
not be terribly upset? How could she not be overtaken by
fright and not run away from it all?

Mary kept silent, thinking. She asked a question and
received the answer. She remained full of meekness and
serenity. Now, if a young girl surrounded by such
extraordinary circumstances is still able to stay emotionally stable, we must be in the presence of a person of exceptional balance. From where did such stability come?
The fact that she was immaculately conceived must have
had a decisive influence because, generally, lack of self-
mastery is the result of sin, that is, of our egoism. In my
opinion, Mary owed her serenity above all to her deep
immersion in the mystery of God, as we shall see later.

It seems to me that no one has ever experienced, the
way Mary did at this moment, such a feeling of utter
loneliness under the enormous weight of a mission imposed by God and before her historical responsibility. In
order to understand exactly what our Lady experienced
at that moment, we will explain what the feeling of loneliness consists in.

To Feel Lonely

All of us have to endure an area of solitude in our personal makeup. This is what makes us different from one another. No one has access to this solitude, and no one ever will.

In decisive moments we are alone.

Only God can descend into these depths, the most remote and distant depths of our beings. Individualization, or consciousness of our personal identity, consists in *being and feeling* that we are different from one another. It is the experience and the sensation of "being there" as conscious and autonomous personality.

Let us imagine a scene: I am on my deathbed in my last agony. Let us suppose that at this moment of suffering I am surrounded by the persons who love me most in this world, who by their presence, words and affection try to *accompany me* at the hour of my passage from life to death. They try to "be with me" at that moment.

In spite of all the consoling words and loving care of these dear ones, at this moment I will "feel alone," totally alone. In this agony no one is or can be with me. The words of my family will reach my ear, but beyond that, where I am different from all others, in the center of my being, I am completely alone, nobody is "with me." Loving manifestations will only touch the surface; in the remote regions of my innermost being no one is with me. No one can *accompany me in my death.* It is a completely personal and solitary experience.

This existential solitude which is so clearly manifest in the example of the agony before death appears also with the same clarity throughout our whole life. If you suffer great sorrow or failure, friends and relatives will surely come to comfort and encourage you. Yet when those friends have gone, you will be left completely alone in carrying the weight of your personal sorrow. No one—except God—can share the burden of your pain. Other human beings can "be with us" to a certain point, but in the real depths of our soul we are absolutely alone.

We experience in a powerful way that same existential solitude at an hour of decision, or of assuming a serious responsibility, or in any important moment of our life. The feeling of being alone, even while accompanied by many counselors, is experienced by all—the father of a family, a doctor, a religious superior, or the president of a nation. Perhaps the loneliest person in the world is the Pope. He can summon advisors, convoke meetings, consult experts, but at the moment of making an important decision he is alone before God and history.

A married couple, at the hour of assuming the responsibility of bringing a person into the world, is alone.

Any of us who hold various degrees of obligation toward persons committed to our care experience deeply that the burden of responsibility is always a burden of solitude: whether in a parish, in the management of a factory, at the head of an organization....

To Choose

With this explanation, we can now understand the gravity of the situation facing Mary at the moment of the annunciation. Mary, an intelligent and reflective young woman, measured her great responsibility. Rising before her like an immense wall was the historical responsibility. She was there, in front of that wall, alone and defenseless. She had been asked a question; she had to answer.

She knew that her future would be determined by her answer. If she responded no, her life would proceed quietly, her children would grow, grandchildren would arrive, and her life would end normally, within the perimeter of the mountains of Nazareth.

If her answer were eventually in the affirmative, it would carry with it all sorts of implications, a genuine chaos would shatter her well-ordered and serene life. To bear a child before marriage implied for her a divorce on the part of Joseph; she could be stoned to death for adultery; she would become socially marginalized and stigmatized with the most offensive name a woman could be given at that time: *harufa*—the raped one.

Beyond these social and human considerations, to be the Mother of the Messiah implied, as Mary well knew, entering the eye of a storm: she would be a sign of contradiction; she would face the flight into Egypt, persecution, tragedy on Calvary, days of sorrow, journeys of suffering.

The Hurdle

The young girl measured the height and the depth of this historic moment. What would her response be?

I am still impressed at how she faced such a responsibility. How is it that under such a tremendous weight she did not break down emotionally? Why did her nerves not give way? Why did she not run away? Above all—a very natural response—why did she not run to her mother for advice: "Mother, I am in a most difficult situation. What must I answer?"

> How could she bear this with integrity, without falling despondent or without later becoming arrogant because she had been chosen among all other human beings?
>
> The burden that had been imposed on her was to be carried in absolute solitude, uncertainty and insecurity, because it regarded something which would occur for the first and only time. And there, in the

face of the great contrast between the poverty of the reality and the splendor of the promise, stood Mary.[5]

One is overwhelmed and awed at the deep humility, at the extraordinary maturity and naturalness with which Mary assumed the Mystery in the midst of immense solitude. The whole of history will not be sufficient to appreciate and admire such grandeur.

It was an indescribable scene. Mary, conscious of the gravity of the moment and of her decision, full of peace, standing alone, without consulting anyone, without having a single manifestation of human support, comes out of herself, makes the great leap, trusts, permits and...*surrenders.*

A cloud of doubts and questions may have fallen upon her: "Is it true that Sarah conceived at the age of ninety? Is it true that my cousin Elizabeth is pregnant at such an advanced age?... But in my case it is beyond all imagining: without human participation! It never happened before. All normal ways have fallen by the wayside. Will it be possible? Nobody must find out about this; I alone will hold the secret in my heart. And if this news did become known, no one would be able to believe or accept it. They would say that I am crazy. When Joseph finds out, what will he say? My God, what do I do? How should I answer?"

The poor girl, solitarily, as an adult in the faith, steps beyond all perplexities and questions, and, full of peace, humility and gentleness, *trusts and surrenders.* "May it be done! I consent, dear Father!"

Mary takes the risk, she says the "yes" of her life without any other motive than her faith and love.

If faith is characterized precisely by a risky decision and solitude under the weight of a burden imposed

by God, the faith of Mary was unique. She is the
prototype of the believer.[6]

Mary is poor and a pilgrim. With her "May it be
done," she enters the great adventure of adult faith. With
this step she burns all her bridges; she cannot turn back.
She is one of the line of Abraham; she is much more than
Abraham on Mount Moria. She is the strong daughter of
the race of pilgrims who feel free because they have
stepped beyond common sense, normal and human rea-
sonings, hurtling themselves into the unfathomable and
fascinating Mystery of the Thrice Holy, repeating tirelessly "Amen," "May it be done." O Paschal Woman!
The people of the Beatitudes have been born, with their
Queen in the lead!

The Servant

"I am the handmaid of the Lord. May it be done to
me according to your word" (Lk 1:38). Again, these are
possibly the most beautiful words in Scripture. It would
certainly be foolish to claim to capture and bring to light
the wealth of profundity contained in this declaration. I
will try to open only a little the doors of this inexhaustible world, placing on the lips of Mary other expressions
accessible to us.

"Angel Gabriel, what do you bring me on behalf of
God? An assignment? A proposition? A demand? If you
are bringing me a demand or proposition, please know
that I have no rights nor can I take any initiative of
my own.

"I am a servant. A servant has no rights. Her rights
are in the hands of her Lord. The task of taking initiative
does not belong to a servant; only that of accepting the
decisions of the Lord.

"Angel Gabriel, tell the Lord to remember that he is *my Lord* and that I am no more than his *poor servant.* Tell him that it is up to him to take the initiative, and to anything he may decide I shall invariably respond: 'It is fine, my Lord!'

"I am one of the *Poor of Yahweh.* I am the poorest creature of the earth; consequently, I am the freest in the world. I have no personal will; the will of my Lord is my will, and the will of all of you is my will. I am the servant of all. In what way can I serve you? I am the First Lady of the world because I am the servant of the world."

Who was Mary? She was that woman who gave her "yes" to her Lord and then was faithful to her decision, to its ultimate consequences and until the end of her life. She was that woman who presented a blank check and extended an infinite and unconditional credit to her Lord God. And never did she retract her word. O faithful woman![7]

May It Be Done to Me

Even grammatically Mary used the passive form. With this declaration she offers herself freely and makes herself available. In this manner Mary manifests a tremendous trust, a bold abandonment into the hands of the Father, accepting all the risks, submitting herself to all the eventualities and crises that the future might bring.

Evely, a Belgian spiritual writer, says that, as in an executive ruling, God presented a proposition and Mary upheld that divine proposal. This interpretation does not convince me. It seems to me that the "May it be done" of Mary entails a fullness and universality much more vast than the accepting of the divine motherhood.

Mary moves according to the spirit of the *poor of Yahweh,* and in this context, in my opinion, our Lady's "May it be done" does not refer directly but rather implicitly to motherhood. After all, divine motherhood constitutes an immortal glory and accepting it is an agreeable and easy task. Her "May it be done," however, embraced much more depth and vastness: it is something like a universal consecration, a self-surrender without reservation or limitation, an acceptance with open arms of any event willed or permitted by the Father, and which she, Mary, will not be able to change.

With her "May it be done," our Lady in fact said "Amen" to the night in Bethlehem, without a house, without a crib, without a midwife—though she would not have had an explicit knowledge of these details; "Amen" to the flight into Egypt, unknown and hostile; "Amen" to the silence of God during the thirty years; "Amen" to the hostility of the Sanhedrin; "Amen" to the political, religious and military forces who had Jesus arrested; "Amen" to the bloodbath of the crucifixion and death; "Amen" to everything the Father arranged or permitted and she could not change.

In a word, Mary, with her "May it be done" entered into the deep and overflowing current of the "Poor of Yahweh," they who never questioned or protested but who surrendered in silence and placed their confidence in the all-powerful and all-loving hands of their dear Lord and Father.

By Way of Contrast

In the Gospel of Luke the adult faith of Mary is like a background melody which glides softly in the midst of a noble symphony. That faith is brilliantly enhanced by an orchestration in which the attitudes of Mary and Zechariah are set against one another.

Elizabeth, on whose home had fallen simultaneously the blessing of a child and the chastisement of

Zechariah who had not believed, says to Mary: "Blessed are you because you believed, dear daughter of Zion; you believed that for God everything is possible; all the marvelous things that have been announced to you will happen exactly as they were announced, in reward for your faith." Instead, here is Zechariah who cannot speak because, due to his unbelief, he remains mute.

To Zechariah it had been announced that they, a couple "advanced in years," were to have a son clothed "in the spirit and power of Elijah" (Lk 1:17-18).

To Mary it was announced that "without knowing man" there would germinate in her solitary womb, in the shadow of the Holy Spirit, a Son who would be great and whose reign would last forever (cf. Lk 1:33).

Zechariah does not believe. "It is impossible," he says. "I am old; my wife is also of advanced age. We are past the time of blossoming. Anyway, Angel Gabriel, give me a sign that all this will happen" (cf. Lk 1:18).

In contrast, Mary neither questions, doubts nor demands a guarantee. With the typical attitude of the *poor of Yahweh*, Mary surrenders in the midst of a complete obscurity, against all hope and evidence (cf. Lk 1:38).

Zechariah, because he did not believe in the word of God, remains mute till the birth of John.

Mary, instead, because she did believe, is transformed into the Mother of God, blessed among women, and proclaimed blessed for generations without end.

That morning, in "that mountainous region of Judah" there was a spiritual feast and in the culminating moment of the feast Mary, Elizabeth and Zechariah must have solemnly repeated in unison the central words of the mystery of faith: "because with God nothing is impossible" (cf. Lk 1:37).

CHAPTER 6

Mary, Before the Silence of God

In this life, in the day-to-day search for the Lord, what is most upsetting to those who walk in faith is the silence of God. "God is the one who, from the beginning of the world, has always been silent: this is the gist of the tragedy," said Unamuno.

Confusion

St. John of the Cross admirably expresses the silence of God in these immortal verses:

Whereto have you hidden yourself,
Beloved, and have left me moaning;
Like the stag you have fled, having wounded me;
I went out for you, shouting, and you had gone.

The conviviality of faith, life with God, is this: an exodus, a perpetual "going out after you, shouting." Here begins the eternal odyssey of the seekers of God; the journey, heavy and monotonous, capable of putting down any resistance; at every moment, in each attempt at prayer, when it seems that the "face" of God is just about to be seen, then "you have gone." The Lord is enwrapped in the veil of silence and remains hidden. He seems a face perpetually in flight, inaccessible, as one who appears and disappears, who is close yet withdraws, concrete yet vanishing.

A Christian is seduced by temptation, and he flounders out of weakness. God is silent. He does not even say a word of reproach. Suppose the opposite: through generous effort, the temptation is overcome. God is still silent: not a word of approval.

You spend the whole night in prayer before the Blessed Sacrament. The entire time you are the only one to speak. The Interlocutor is silent. What is more, when in the morning you leave the church, tired and drowsy, you will not hear a kind word of gratitude or courtesy. The whole night, the Other is silent, and at the time of parting he is still silent.

If you go into a garden, you will see that the flowers speak, the birds speak, even the stars speak. Only God is silent. It is said that creatures speak of God, but God himself is quiet. The whole universe is an immense, profound evocation of the Mystery, but the Mystery itself vanishes in silence.

Suddenly the star disappears from the view of the Magi kings, and they are completely at a loss. Jesus on the cross experiences a powerful interior sensation that he is alone, that the Father is absent, that the Father has also abandoned him.

❖

All of a sudden the universe around us is full of enigmas and questions. ...How many years did this mother have? Thirty-two, and now she is dying of cancer, leaving six small children behind her. How can this be? ...She was a beautiful three-year-old child. Meningitis leaves her an invalid for the rest of her life. ...The whole family died in a car accident one Sunday after-

noon, on their way back from the beach. How is it possible? ...A slanderous act against a frustrated worker has
thrown him out on the street, without his reputation and
without employment. Where was God? ...The man had
nine children, he was fired by an arbitrary, brutal boss,
the whole family is without a house and without food.
Does justice exist? And those gorgeous mansions, so
close to a hillside ugly with miserable shacks. What is the
Lord doing? Is he not a Father? Why is he silent?

It is an obstinate and intolerable silence which slowly undermines the most solid characters. Confusion sets
in. Voices begin to surge—from where you do not
know—and they call for an answer. "Where is your
God?" (Ps 42:4) This is not sarcasm coming from a disciple of Voltaire, nor is it a formal argument voiced by an
intellectual atheist.

The believer is invaded by the unrelieved and disconcerting silence of God. Little by little he is dominated
by a vague sense of insecurity: he asks himself if what he
knows about God is all true, if it is not merely the product of his mind, or if, on the contrary, it is not the most
solid of all realities. And there he is sailing on rough
waters, upset by the silence of God. Is this not what
Psalm 30 says so bluntly? "When you hid your face I was
terrified" (v. 8).

The prophet Jeremiah experienced this silence of
God with a terrifying vividness. He says to the Lord:
"Yahweh God, after what I have endured for you all of
my life, mockeries and attacks, could it be that you are
no more than a mirage, a simple vapor of water?" (cf.
Jer 15:15-18)

Only a profound spirit of abandonment and an
adult faith will deliver us from being upset and help us
to not be broken by this silence. Adult faith is that which

sees the essential and the invisible. It is that faith which "knows" that behind the silence God breathes and that behind the mountains dawn will appear. That which is essential always remains hidden from the human retina, be it the retina of the eye or of the heart. The essential and ultimate reality remains accessible only to the penetrating glance of pure and naked faith, of an adult faith.

Walking in Faith

Let us look at the behavior of Mary before the silence of God.

Nazareth is about 130 miles from Bethlehem. In Mary's time that distance must have seemed much greater.

> The roads of the country had not as yet been traced and attended by the Romans who were masters in such matters. They were bad roads, scarcely passable by caravans of donkeys and camels.
>
> In the best of cases, all that travelers could make use of was a donkey to transport food and necessities, one of those donkeys that you see even today in Palestine following a group of people on foot.[8]

We do not know if Mary had to present herself for the census; it seems unlikely. The fact is that Joseph went to Bethlehem "with Mary, his betrothed, who was with child" (Lk 2:5).

> These words could very well imply a delicate allusion to one of the reasons Mary made the trip also: that is, the proximity of the birth, a circumstance in which it was not proper to leave her behind alone.[9]

Mary could not travel in a caravan due to her state of pregnancy. The caravans advanced with a certain rapidity which a pregnant woman in her ninth month could not have endured. Sitting on a donkey, Mary had to travel slowly, stopping at various places for rest in the company of Joseph. Due to her condition the trip was certainly slow and tiring. We can calculate that under such circumstances it must have taken them eight to ten days to finally arrive at their destination.

The rainy season in Palestine begins in November. The roads must have been muddy with puddles and partially impassable in some stretches. Mary and Joseph most likely suffered from cold the whole way, especially in the plains beaten by the strong winds coming from Mount Hermon.

❖

Again we must put ourselves into a contemplative mood so as to enter into Mary's interior, to monitor the pulse of her heart and admire her inner beauty.

Poor and dignified, the young mother-to-be advances on her difficult journey. Today, cold and rain render the walk particularly uncomfortable. But Mary is a *servant*, she has no right to protest. Within the spirituality of the *Servant of the Lord* she responds to the inclement weather: "It is all right, Father. *May it be done.*" She remains full of peace in spite of the rain and the cold.

The psychology of the young woman who is to become a mother for the first time is amazing: she lives between joy and fear. The silence of God, as a dark sky full of questions, swoops over her: "When will the birth pangs begin?" In those times every delivery brought the danger of death. "Will there be complications, or will everything go smoothly and well?" Nobody knows. "Will we arrive at Bethlehem in time? And if the birth happens on the way, before we arrive, what shall we do? Will there be a woman of experience who could help me at that moment?"

No one knows anything. God continues to be silent. Facing these and other questions, Mary is not angry or anxious. Peacefully she answers once and always: *"Let it be.* I consent, Father. I abandon myself to you." Never was there seen on this earth a woman of such peace, fortitude, gentleness and elegance.

"Where will we sleep tonight? There, in one of the bends of the road, or at the foot of this hill? Let's go to that spot out there." What looked comfortable from afar is a hollow of mud and wind. "Is there not a better place? Night is falling; it is too late to look for another place; therefore we have no choice but to sleep, or sleep badly, in the damp and manure."

God does not give any sign of life. In accordance with her spirituality Mary does not fail to say: "My Lord, we did all we could to find a good place; you have permitted that we should remain here for the night. It is fine, Father. *Let it be so.* I embrace your will." This heroic "May it be done" will help Mary never to break down emotionally, and will keep her free from all anxiety.

Days pass. Mary and Joseph do all that is possible to procure nourishment and rest. Whenever the results fall short, Mary does not resist nor get agitated. She surrenders. "They had to sleep in public resting places along the road among camels and donkeys."[10] God remained silent. What will Mary do?

She will not cry because such tears are a kind of protest and the servant of the Lord cannot protest, she can only accept. Her "Let it be" will forever give her a formidable interior state of calm, serenity and dignity, far beyond the average. There will never be any sorrowful tragedy or surprising event which will disturb Mary's emotional stability. Before becoming our Lady, she was the Lady of her own soul.

An Unshakable Gentleness

They arrived at Bethlehem. At a set moment Luke says "there was no room for them in the inn" (Lk 2:7). From this fact we shall draw some most interesting details for our contemplation.

That "inn" of which Luke speaks was simply the lodging destined for caravans, the actual Palestinian *Khan.*

> It is an enclosure without a roof, protected by a high wall, with only one door....
>
> The beasts were in the center, in the open air, and the travelers under the porches or among the animals.
>
> And in this jumble of men and beasts they talked about business, they prayed, they sang, they slept, they ate; some could be born there, others could die.[11]

The evangelist says that there was no room "for them" in the caravan inn. Riciotti, an Italian scholar, explains that this phrase is laden with meaning. As for a place, they could have found one in any one of these lodgings. No innkeeper would say that there was no room.[12] There was room, physically speaking. But adding "for them" alluded to the fact that the place was not adequate for an imminent childbirth. Otherwise, the evangelist would have said, simply, that there was no room.

This means that at a certain moment Mary along with Joseph had gone to take stock of the caravan inn. But when Mary heard the turmoil of shouts coming from men as well as from animals, she was horrified at the thought that the delivery could be the object of the general curiosity of so many people; she preferred any other place, though uncomfortable and damp, if only it could be solitary and reserved.

These are two historical reasons why Jesus was born in a grotto: poverty and purity. Poverty, because had they been rich all doors would have been opened to them. Purity in this case consisted of discretion, dignity and modesty, qualities which always appear to adorn Mary. The delicate Mother preferred a quiet though inconvenient place, as long as it kept her away from the curiosity of other people at the hour of birth. In particular, then, these two jewels shine on the forehead of the young Mother.

Riciotti puts it this way: "Mary wished to surround her childbirth with a reverent reserve."

What we have just analyzed can be said about other situations. If Mary, as a last resort, intended to look for a corner in the caravan inn, then they must have exhausted all other possibilities in looking for a small space in the homes of relatives, friends or acquaintances who surely could afford to grant them space. To abandon oneself to the will of the Father does not mean to cross one's arms and wait without doing all one can to resolve the problems; but rather at the time of the results, whatever they are, to abandon oneself into the hands of the Father. Without a doubt, this is what Mary did.

> Popular imagination has given way to moving scenes: Mary and Joseph go from door to door; from one they are sent to another.... The Gospels say nothing in this regard. But something like this must have occurred.... It would have been the most natural thing to do.[13]

Again we enter into Mary's interior. Providence gives no sign. Securing a place is urgent. The birth pangs can begin at any moment.

Each time they knock at the door of a relative or acquaintance they experience both a hope and a letdown:

the hope that perhaps they will be granted a place for the delivery, and a letdown because in the end the doors are closed, even if amiably.

Mary was young. She had not been exposed as yet to the blows of life. Because of her age she was very sensitive. She was also sensitive by temperament, as we shall see in another part of this book. In addition, her state of emotion and fear—felt by every woman on the eve of giving birth for the first time—would surely aggravate this sensitivity.

They called on other acquaintances, other relatives, other friends. All doors were shut on them, all horizons and hopes were closed. The bravest of women would have broken down. But in this case the most cruel circumstances could not disturb the interior equilibrium of this young woman. Again and again her "May it be done" would free her from anxiety and emotional breakdown; it would confer on her an indestructible fortitude and leave her in a state of deep calm, gentleness, dignity and grandeur. Quietly, she would go on searching for other homes and other solutions.

When all possibilities were exhausted, with no indications given from the silent Lord, Mary and Joseph went again to see whether they would find some small space in the various inns for caravans. Less satisfied than ever, they finally decided to go up the mountain to find a quiet and discreet place.

This is how the servant of the Lord surrendered indefectibly into the hands of the Father, how she waited with an unshakable gentleness for the great moment.

The Fugitive Mother

Then, one day, the Lord spoke: "Rise, take the child and his mother, flee to Egypt, and stay there until I tell you" (Mt 2:13). These few words brought a flood of questions to Mary's heart.

"Why is Herod searching for this Child? How did he find out about his birth? What wrong has he committed? Why does the king want to get rid of him? Flee to Egypt? Why not Samaria, Syria or Lebanon where Herod does not rule? How are we to survive there? What language will we speak? In which temple shall we worship? How long will we have to stay there? How long before God will tell us otherwise? Are the persecutors close?"

Again the terrible silence of God fell upon the young Mother like a dark cloud. How many times the same thing happens in our own lives. Suddenly, everything seems absurd. Nothing makes sense. Everything seems a blind and sinister fate. We feel like mere playthings in the midst of a whirlwind. God? If he exists and is all powerful, why does he permit all this? Why is he silent? We feel like rebelling, denying the whole thing.

Mary does not rebel, she abandons herself. To every problem she answers her "May it be done." A servant does not ask questions, she surrenders. "My Lord, I abandon myself in silence into your hands. Do with me what you will. I am ready for anything. I accept everything. I shall fight with every fiber of my being for the safety of the Child and for my own life. But during the struggle and after I will place my destiny in your hands." Thus Mary, in silence and peace, undertakes the flight into a strange land.

❖

At this moment Mary entered into the condition of a political fugitive. The existence of this Child threatened the security of a throne. And the king, for his own security, threatened the life of the Child, who had to flee in the arms of his Mother to guarantee his survival.

To know Mary's state of mind during this escape, we must understand the psychology of a political fugitive. A political fugitive lives from one fright to another. He cannot sleep in the same place two successive nights. Every unfamiliar person is a potential informer. Any suspect is a police officer in civilian clothes. A fugitive lives dangerously, always on the defensive.

Thus Mary lived during that time, from one fright to another: "Those people behind us, would they be Herod's agents? Those coming toward us? Who are these people ahead of us? Those who have stopped just now? Should we sleep here tonight? What is better, to travel by day or by night?"

Another element of the flight—one realized in the psychology of every fugitive—was the need to move slowly yet in haste. Slowly because they could not travel by the main roads where they might be spotted by Herod's men; rather, they had to wind their way around the hills and secondary roads, through Hebron, Beersheba and Idumea. And in haste so as to leave Herod's kingdom as soon as possible and cross the border of El-Arish.

> On approaching the delta of the Nile we come into the classic desert called the 'Sea of Sand,' in which there are no shrubs, nor a single blade of grass, nor any stones; nothing but sand.

> The three fugitives had to drive themselves with great fatigue during the day across moving sands and in stifling heat, spend the night sleeping on the sand; they had nothing but the little water and scarce food they had brought with them, just enough for a week.

> If a modern traveler should follow the same route, he would have to spend various sleepless nights in the open air in this desolate part of Idumea. During

the day he might see a small group of men pass by, and even a woman with a child at her breast; he would notice how taciturn and dreamy they appear, as if resigned to their fate, gazing toward an unknown destination.

Whoever has had such an experience and made such encounters in that desert has contemplated not just scenes of local color, but a sort of historical document about the trip of the three fugitives from Bethlehem.[14]

In the midst of this barren, devastating solitude, surrounded by the most impressive silence of God, the fugitive Mother journeys, a heartrending figure, yet with the air of a great lady, humble, abandoned to the hands of the Father, full of an unshakable gentleness, repeating unceasingly her "Amen" while trying not to be discovered by the police.

The Trial of Erosion

Among the most renowned and effective tactics in destroying a person or an institution, is what could be called "the psychological war of erosion." It is said that a drop of water falling on the same spot can erode solid rock. To be a hero for a week or a month is relatively easy, because it is exciting. But to resist breakdown under the monotony of years is much more difficult.

In my opinion, the most acute trial for Mary's faith was on Calvary, but the more dangerous trial was the thirty years under the vault of the silence of God. The wound inflicted by the "sword" (cf. Lk 2:35), though it must have been most cruel and bloody, was not as threatening to the emotional stability of Mary's faith as the interminable thirty years which surrounded her soul with routine and erosion. To understand the dangerous journey Mary traveled during these thirty years, we will recall some parallel cases.

❖

According to the Bible, Abraham was promised a son in his seventy-fifth year. But God, in his divine plan, was to delay the accomplishment of his promise and subject Abraham's faith to the trial of erosion. Years passed and the child did not arrive, and the soul of Abraham began to pine. More years passed and the son did not come; Abraham's faith began to waver to the point that he fell into a deep depression. So as not to falter completely he demanded from God a guarantee, a visible phenomenon, a sign (cf. Gen 15:8).

Halfway through the last century, in Lourdes, France, Bernadette Soubirous had an extraordinary series of heavenly manifestations. Then suddenly the heavens became silent, and until the day of her death, this silence accompanied her. Her biographers say that this silence was so upsetting to Bernadette that she began to have serious doubts about the reality of the long-passed apparitions.

It is always the same: the more intense the light of the sun, the deeper the shadows. The more resounding the manifestation of God, the deeper will his silence be afterwards. This is what occurred in the case of Mary. Let us contemplate this phenomenon in her life.

❖

Years were passing. The deep and fresh impression of the annunciation was beginning to fade into the past; it was no more than a dull memory, like a distant echo. Mary felt as though she were caught between ancient promises and the present realities, opaque and meaningless. The monotony took flesh in Nazareth, among unchanging geographical horizons and among human horizons that also seemed to be paralyzed.

The monotony always had the same face: long hours, long days, an interminable thirty years. Neighbors shut themselves into their homes. In winter it gets dark quite early: doors and windows are closed; Jesus and Mary remain face to face. The Mother observes everything: the Son is there—he works, he eats, he prays. Always the same, day after day, week after week, each year seems to be an eternity. The impression is that everything is in a rut, everything is always the same, like a monotonous wasteland.

What was the Mother doing? In the everlasting hours, while Mary was grinding the wheat, kneading the bread, carrying wood from the hill or water from the spring, she was turning over in her mind the words that one day—such a long time ago—she had heard the angel say: "He will be great, and will be called Son of the Most High,...and of his kingdom there will be no end" (Lk 1:32-33). These ancient words were resplendent, yet the reality before her eyes was so different: the young lad, working in an obscure corner of the rustic home, silent, solitary, reserved.... He will be great? He was not great, he was just the same as all the others.

Perplexity began to knock insistently at the doors of Mary's mind. Could all of this be true? Was I the victim of a hallucination? Were those words simply dreams of human grandeur?

❖

This is the supreme temptation in our life of faith: to want evidence, to want to grasp reality with our hands, to perceive it as though it were physical, to attempt to step from moving sands to firm ground, to want to jump out of the obscure night, to open our eyes and see the sun, or to say to the Lord: "Incomparable Father, give me a proof to assure me that everything is true; transform yourself before my eyes into a fire, a tempest or a hurricane."

Mary did not do that. Shaken by the perplexity, she did not become agitated. She remained quiet, she abandoned herself unconditionally, without resistance, into the arms of monotony as an expression of the will of the Father. When everything seemed absurd, she responded "Amen" to what was so absurd, and the absurdity disappeared. To the silence of God she answered, "Let it be," and silence was transformed into presence. Instead of demanding a guarantee of veracity, Mary clung indefatigably to the will of God; she remained in peace, and doubt turned into sweetness.

Social life in Nazareth was inexorably monotonous. Reports about nationalistic agitations and imperialist repressions reached Nazareth as a late and muffled echo with no punch, nor would such reports challenge or bother the Nazarenes.

The young man is now 15, 18, 20 years old; there is no manifestation, all is silent, nothing is new. This is a great danger for Mary's faith. She could be shattered by discouragement or by the complete void. But she does not open the doors to doubt: "Could all of this be true? It seems that I made a mistake."

❖

Now the Son is an adult of 22, 25, 28 years. His relative John, the son of Zechariah, is shaking the capital, Jerusalem, drawing multitudes to the desert. And Jesus? There he is: he scarcely speaks, he goes to houses to fix a window, a table, a chair; he climbs to the roof to repair a rafter, he brings home tree trunks to make yokes. His Mother observes, meditates and remains silent. The Son does not prepare himself for any kind of mission. Besides, nothing new seems to be in the making. The young man is the same as others of his age. The words of the annunciation definitely seem the beautiful dreams of a summer night.

And she? Had she not been told that all generations would call her blessed? Impossible. She was nearing the sunset years of life. She appeared prematurely old as always happens with persons of underdeveloped countries. Her life, apparently, was not much different from that of her neighbors. It had been so many years since something special had occurred to her, and, seemingly, nothing new could be discerned on the horizon of her life. At times, everything appeared so empty, so meaningless.... I am sure that Mary's faith was assaulted and dashed by a flood of questions which broke upon her in successive waves.

So as not to succumb, Mary had to display an enormous amount of mature faith, pure and naked faith, which rests on God himself.

Her secret was this: not to resist but to surrender. Mary could not change anything—not the delayed manifestation of Jesus, nor the routine which like a shadow was enveloping and invading everything, nor the upsetting silence of God.... If she could not change any of this, why should she resist? The Father wished it that way or permitted it. "Therefore, Father, I abandon myself to you."

Only the development of a great intimacy with the Father and her unwavering abandonment into his hands freed Mary from worse dangers on her pilgrimage. In this way Mary lived the passage of those thirty years, navigating in the barque of mature faith.

❖

The same experience occurs in religious life or in the priesthood: the priestly anointing was received, the vows of profession were pronounced. In the first years everything was new. The initial generosity helped these persons to unfold powerful energies, harvesting brilliant results which, in turn, fed their enthusiasm. But after some fifteen or twenty years, the novelty wore off. Without knowing how, and without anyone noticing it, routine crept into everything, like an invisible shadow: in the office, parish, college, hospital, chapel, and above all...in life itself. Then fatigue showed up, and it became more difficult to be faithful and much more difficult to "shine brightly like the splendor of the firmament" (Dn 12:3).

It happens in marriage, too. The novelty and freshness of the first years, anticipation for the first child, are able to sustain the flame of new love. But what happens afterwards? With the passing of years the spouses move unvaryingly within the closed circle of their unchanging horizons, monotony begins to invade everything, routine replaces the novelty, and little by little the crises begin to threaten, sometimes quite seriously, the stability of the marriage.

For any person or situation, Mary is the model. Her courage and strength, her mature faith will free us from any suffocating circumstance.

A Sword

When the Council tells us that Mary was advancing on the pilgrimage of faith, it speaks with insistence, in the same paragraph, about what happened on Calvary:

"[She] faithfully persevered in her union with her Son unto the cross, where she stood, in keeping with the divine plan, grieving exceedingly with her only begotten Son, uniting herself with a maternal heart with his sacrifice, and lovingly consenting to the immolation of this Victim which she herself had brought forth" (LG 58). Through these expressions and, above all, their context, the Council seems to indicate that the culminating moment for the faith of the Mother—and also the trial, for there is no greatness without trial—occurred on Calvary.

There is another paragraph in the same document in which the Council, with a succinct and moving description, magnifies the faith of Mary at its highest expression, there, near the cross.

In fact, speaking of the "May it be done" that Mary pronounced on the day of the annunciation, the Council adds these significant words: "She sustained [her "May it be done"] without wavering beneath the cross...." (LG 62). Thus the Council desires to indicate that the most difficult trial for Mary's "May it be done" was the catastrophe of Calvary.

Without leaving the spirit of the conciliar text I would like to present here a few reflections which should redound to the greatest glory of Mary.

❖

Possibly the most all-embracing and sorrowful event in the Bible is summarized in these laconic words: "Standing by the cross of Jesus were his mother..." (Jn 19:25). These brief words evoke a vast universe, with transcendental implications for the history of salvation.

In another part of this book we speak about the spiritual motherhood which is born here at the foot of the cross. Now our interest is to focus our contemplation exclusively from the point of view of faith.

The key question that will weigh the merit and consequently the grandeur of Mary's faith is this: Did Mary realize the total significance of what was happening that afternoon on Calvary? Did she know, for example, all that we have come to know about the far-reaching and redemptive significance of that bloody death?

Ambiguous positions are held about this matter. To clarify the issue somewhat, we would have to ask other questions, for example: If Mary knew everything, was her merit greater or lesser? If she penetrated into the Mystery for only a glimmering instant, would the merit of her faith increase or diminish? Can we affirm, in some sense, that the less knowledge she had, the more meritorious and great was her faith? Many conclusions will depend on the mental presuppositions that each one may have regarding the person of Mary. I too have thoughts on this question and I believe they throw a most illuminating light on Mary's faith.

In any event, before we move ahead we must clearly distinguish in Mary the theological knowledge she may have had at Calvary from her faith. Greatness does not belong to Mary because of her knowledge, whether greater or lesser, but because of her faith.

❖

To know exactly what happened to Mary on that afternoon, we cannot imagine her as an abstract and solitary being, isolated from those around her, but as a normal person who receives the influential impact of her surroundings. Thus we are as human beings, and so undoubtedly was Mary.

Now, from the evangelical context, the death of Jesus seemed like a final catastrophe to the apostles. It was the end of everything. That impression and state of mind are clearly depicted in the scene on the road to Emmaus. Cleopas, after showing his grief because his Interlocutor was ignorant of the recent events which were for him a fresh and deep wound, concluded by saying: "We had hoped...," like one who wishes to add: "but everything is lost"; as if all was but a beautiful dream; that's what it was, a dream!

Caiaphas, representing the opposite side, had the conviction that once it was over for Jesus, so it was for the movement. He was right, because this is exactly what happened. When the apostles saw Jesus in the hands of his enemies, they forgot about their oaths of fidelity, and each one, trying to save his own skin, took to flight, separated, and abandoned the whole business. Three days later they were still hiding, with the doors well bolted (cf. Jn 20:19) so as to feel safe, now that they had lost their leader.

This was their state of mind: he was sleeping in his sepulcher, buried forever. "We had a beautiful dream, but now it is buried with the Dreamer." This explains their obstinate resistance in believing the news of the resurrection. On the day of Pentecost the Holy Spirit clarified the whole panorama of Jesus. It was only then that they knew who Jesus Christ was.

❖

And Mary? First, we must not forget that she was part of this group of people so confused and dejected.

I cannot imagine Mary adoring every drop of blood that flowed from the cross. I would not imagine that she knew the entire theology of the redemption achieved through Jesus' death, a theology that the Holy Spirit taught us beginning with Pentecost.

If she had known all that we know, what would her merit have been? In the midst of this scene it would have been for her an immense consolation to know that only one drop of this blood would have sufficed to save the world; to know that if the Son was lost, the world and history were being gained; to know, besides, that the absence of the Son was only for a short time. In these circumstances, it would have cost her little to peacefully accept this death.

Neither can I imagine her defeated by the total dispersion of the apostles, thinking that everything ended there. By no means.

We see in the Gospel that Mary was navigating between lights and shadows, at times understanding most clearly, at other times less, meditating on the ancient words and adhering to the will of the Father, perceiving slowly but progressively the transcendent mystery of Jesus Christ. According to the Gospels, Mary was walking in faith.

❖

This being so, what did happen on Calvary?

Although this is a difficult task, I will attempt to enter into the Mother's vital situation, and demonstrate what her supreme greatness consisted in at that moment.

Mary is engulfed in the encircling winds of a violent tempest, interpreted by everybody as being the final disaster of a golden project.

We need to imagine the human surroundings that Mary was standing in the center of: in the foreground, the executors of the sentence, cold and indifferent; a little

farther, the triumphant Sanhedrin; still farther, the multitude of curious bystanders among whom we see a few
valiant women, powerless and in tears, showing their
sympathy for the Crucified One. For all these groups
without exception, what was happening was the ultimate scene of a tragedy.

Dreams were ending here along with the Dreamer.

We must place ourselves in the center of this vital
and fateful circle wherein some were mourning, others
celebrating this sad finale. In the middle of this whirlwind, we find the dignified and pathetic figure of Mary,
clinging to her faith so as not to break down emotionally,
understanding some things, for example, the "sword,"
perceiving others only in a confused manner.... These
were not moments for beautiful theologies. When one
is tossed about by a hurricane all one wants to do is to
remain on one's feet without falling.

To understand? To know? This is not what is important. Mary did not understand the words of the twelve-
year-old Child; nevertheless even there her reaction was
sublime. The important thing is not the knowledge but
the faith, and surely, here the faith of Mary climbed the
highest of mountains. Could she who had not understood the words of Simeon (cf. Lk 2:33), understand completely what was happening on Calvary? The important
thing was not to understand, but to surrender.

❖

In the midst of this obscurity, Mary, says the Council, (cf. LG 62) maintained her "May it be done" on a high
and sustained pitch.

"Heavenly Father, I scarcely understand anything
in this general confusion; all I understand is that had you

not wanted this it would never have happened. Then, may it be done *according to your will.*

"Everything seems incomprehensible, but I consent, Father. I cannot see why he should have died so young, and above all, in this way, but I accept your will. It is fine, dear Father.

"I do not see that it had to be this chalice and no other to save the world. But that is not important. It is enough for me to know that it is your will. Let it be. The important thing is not to see but to accept.

"I do not see why the One awaited for such a long time had to be interrupted so soon at the beginning of his work. One day you told me that my Son would be great. I do not see that he is great. But, in spite of the fact that I see nothing, I know that everything is all right. I accept all, I consent to everything. May your will be done!

"Father dear, into your arms I place my beloved Son."

The holocaust was perfect, the oblation total. Mary acquired a spiritual and sublime perfection. Never was she so poor and so great. She seemed to be a pale shadow near the cross, but at the same time she had the stature of a queen.

That evening, the Faithful One raised an altar on the highest peak of the world.

❖

Our Lady of Easter:
Our Lady of the Cross and of Hope,
Our Lady of Friday and of Sunday,
Our Lady of the night and of the morning,
Our Lady of all departures,
because you are the Lady
of the "transit" or of the "pasch."

Hear us:
Today we wish to tell you, "thank you very much."
Thanks so much, Lady, for your "Fiat";
for your complete availability as a "slave,"
for your poverty and your silence.

For the joy of your seven swords.
For the grief of all your departures,
that have given peace to so many hearts.
For having remained with us,
in spite of time and distances.

—*Cardinal Pironio*

PART THREE
SILENCE

"For when peaceful stillness compassed everything
and the night in its swift course was half spent,
Your all-powerful word from heaven's royal throne
bounded, a fierce warrior, into the doomed land...."
—Wisdom 18:14-16

The heart knows what the tongue
will never utter and what the ears can never hear.
—Gibran

CHAPTER 7

Fidelity in Silence

All that is definitive is born and consummated in the midst of silence: life, death, the hereafter, grace, sin. What throbs is always hidden.

Silence is the new name of God. He penetrates everything; he creates, preserves and sustains all things and no one realizes it. If we did not have his Word and experience proofs of his loving care every day, we would say that God *is* silence, he always was and always will be. He works silently in the depths of our souls.

In the inexplicable designs of his initiative, free and liberating, the operations of his grace are born. Why does he give to some and not to others? Why now and not later? Why in this degree and not in another? All remains in silence. Gratuity, by definition, has neither reasons nor explanations. It is silence.

This is why our God is disconcerting, because he is essentially gratuitous. Everything comes from him—grace and glory, merit and reward. Nothing is deserved, everything is received. He loved us first. No one can question his decisions. No human being can stand before him and claim, demand or question. Everything is grace. This explains why his ways are upsetting and frequently plunge us into confusion.

At times we have the impression that the Father has abandoned us. But just around the corner he suddenly envelops us with an inebriating visitation. Though his normal ways are the ordinary channels of his grace, all of a sudden he surprises us with unexpected gifts. God is like this. We must accept him as he is.

There is no "human" logic in his actions. His thoughts and judgments are different from ours. The most difficult task is to be patient with our God. The most difficult part of our ascension to him is to accept his essential gratuity peacefully, to endure his delays patiently, to accept in silence realities that he fosters and permits. This is God—pure gratuity.

❖

His grace acts in silence. It filters silently into the most complex openings of human nature. Nobody knows how it happens. The genetic code, biochemical combinations, traumas of childhood or those inflicted while in the womb—nobody knows whether these factors obstruct or destroy our freedom, the soil in which the tree of grace casts its roots.

Sin? It is the supreme mystery of silence. Who can weigh it? Fidelity is a duel between grace and freedom. Who can measure it? To what degree does grace put pressure on us, and to what degree does our free will resist grace? All remains in silence, without answer.

In human behavior, how much is due to a genetic inclination inherited from our parents, how much has been determined by the "wounds" of infancy, and how much is the fruit of a free act of the will? Everything remains without an answer.

Let us look around us. We haughtily condemn someone because they have had a violent fit of anger or because they were the cause of public scandal by something they did. Everyone has witnessed the angry explosion or scandal, and all feel the right to judge and condemn. But who was present before to witness the person's spiritual victories? Who knows about the dozen times when, before that sin, they did gain victory over anger in the silence of the heart? All of us are aware of the generosity and perseverance we displayed, of how many defeats we registered before we felt some progress in humility, patience, maturity, and of how many more efforts we need before others can notice our progress.

Why do some triumph and others fail? Why has this fellow with a brilliant mind been a failure all of his life? Why has this other rather mediocre person emerged above the others? Who would have thought that this child, born in an obscure corner of the world, would leave such a deep mark on history? Who would have dreamed that this person or political movement would meet with such failure? Everything is covered with a veil. Everything is silence.

❖

All that is permanent bears the seal of silence. How many of his contemporaries perceived even a glimpse of the immortal substantial presence of the eternal God in the obscure Nazarene called Jesus? With what eyes was he contemplated by Philip, Nathanael or Andrew? What did Nicodemus or Caiaphas think of him?

The Son of God's crossing over the deep waters of humanity was done in complete silence. One who contemplates this event remains dumbfounded. A meteor flashes across the skies silently but at least it is brilliant. God, during his passage through human experience, did not even shine: he was an eclipse, pure silence. What amazes us most in Jesus and his Mother is their silent humility.

How many were aware that this neighbor carrying wood or water, who never meddled in the affairs of others but who helped them when it was needed—how many knew that this neighbor was "full of grace," highly favored by the Lord, and far above all other women of the earth?

What did her relatives in Cana or her close family think of her? The whole mystery of Mary was enwrapped in the folds of silence during the major part of her life. Many of her privileges, such as the Immaculate Conception, the Assumption, were enveloped in silence for many centuries even in the Church. We return to the same conclusion: all that is permanent, definitive, remains in silence.

Receptivity

I have chosen this word, "silence," for the title of this book and of this chapter because it seemed to me that this word summarizes and expresses Mary's history and personality exactly.

There are expressions in the Bible which are laden with an extraordinary vitality. Our modern languages do not possess words that can absorb and transmit that same richness of meaning. Take as an example the word "shalom." Our "peace" does not do justice to the richness of the Hebrew expression. "Anau" means much more than our word "poor." The simple word "faith," which Paul speaks so much about, contains richer overtones than the same word on our lips.

Similarly, when I use the word "silence" as applied to Mary, I wish to evoke a complex prism of repercussions.

When speaking of silence in the case of Mary, I am thinking of her availability and receptivity. In speaking of the *silence of Mary,* I wish to evoke expressions like depth, fullness, fecundity; ideas like fortitude, self-mastery, human maturity, but especially the words *fidelity* and *humility.* I would consider these almost synonyms of silence.

Place of Birth

She is called Mary of Nazareth. The name of Nazareth does not appear even once in the Old Testament, nor in the Talmud. In his two famous works, *Jewish Antiquities* and *The Jewish War,* Flavius Josephus exhausts all of the geographical and historical material on Palestine. In no part of these books does the name of Nazareth appear.

As we well know, the Romans noted carefully in their maps of the Empire the names of the towns and cities of their vast territories, even the names of the most insignificant places. The name of Nazareth does not appear on any of these lists.

Nazareth "is" silence.

The only writings that speak of Nazareth are the Gospels. It is interesting to note the evangelist recalls the irony of Nathanael, so typical among provincial rival towns: "Can anything good come from Nazareth?" (Jn 1:46)

She is called Mary of Nazareth. Nazareth is anonymous. Mary, by birth, "is" silence and anonymity.

❖

We do not know when or where Mary was born, nor who her parents were. We do not know when or where she died, nor if she died. All is silence around Mary.

About any important personage, the first interesting detail is to know the time and place of birth. For the date of Mary's birth we can only make an approximate guess, on the basis of certain customs of that time, as, for example, the age of "betrothal."

We cannot even guess Mary's birthplace because in a region of semi-nomadic customs the inhabitants do not choose a stable place to live. For any motive they move from one place to another, settle themselves temporarily in yet another place, and their children are born anywhere. Mary could have been born in Naim, Bethsaida or Cana. No one knows.

The same can be said of her parents. Tradition tells us they were Joachim and Ann, but that comes from the apocryphal gospels. The canonical Gospels say nothing in this regard. All is uncertain, nothing is sure. The origins of Mary are hidden in the most obscure silence.

❖

An impressive silence envelops the life of Mary in the Bible. In the Gospels Mary comes on the scene incidentally and then immediately disappears.

The first two chapters tell us about her. But even here, Mary appears like a chandelier; the important one is the Light, the Child. As we have already said, information about the infancy has come to us, ultimately, from Mary. In a certain sense we could say: here, Mary speaks. She speaks of Joseph, of Zechariah, of Simeon, of the shepherds, of the angels, of the kings.... About herself she hardly says anything. Mary is not narcissistic.

Later in the Gospels, Mary appears and disappears like a shooting star, as though there were a kind of shame in presenting her: in the Temple when the Child was lost (cf. Lk 2:41-50); in Cana (cf. Jn 2:1-12); in Capernaum (cf. Mk 3:31-35); on Calvary (cf. Jn 19:25-28); in the Cenacle, presiding over the group of the Twelve in prayer (cf. Acts 1:14). In these last three scenes Mary does not even say a word.

Afterwards, we meet with one indirect, much more impersonal allusion: "born of a woman." Here Paul refers to Mary in a strangely anonymous manner: "God sent his Son, born of a woman" (Gal 4:4). It would have been easy to place the name of Mary after the word "woman." It would have been natural. But no, Mary's destiny is to always remain in the background, in the penumbra of silence.

We cannot but be impressed by the little importance Paul seemingly gives to Mary. Chronologically speaking, the two could have known each other personally, and probably did. In claiming his apostolic authority Paul glorifies himself for personally knowing James, the "brother" of Jesus (cf. Gal 1:19). Nevertheless, he makes no mention of Mary in his letters.

❖

Apart from these appearances, the Bible says nothing more about Mary. The rest is silence. Only God is important. Mary is transparent, and remains in silence.

Mary was like a large window, clean and transparent. Let us imagine that we are in a house, sitting in an armchair, contemplating various scenes and beautiful landscapes: people strolling on the street, trees and birds, splendid panoramas, stars in the night. Before such beauty our enthusiasm knows no bounds. But to whom do we owe all this? Who realizes the presence and function of the windowpane? If, instead of glass, we had a wall, would we see these marvelous things? The window is so humble that it silently lets the exterior beauty enter into our life.

This is exactly what Mary did.

She was, like the window, so pure, so spotless, so disinterested and humble that she let the whole mystery of God and his salvation come through her, while she remained in silence. Hardly anyone in the Bible realized her presence.

Sailing on the sea of anonymity, lost in the night of silence, always open to sacrificing herself, always a sign of hope, the figure of the Mother is not that of a "great personality" with its own characteristics.

This is the destiny of Mary. Rather, Mary had no destiny; nor did she have traits specific to her. She was always adorned with the figure of the Son. She was always related to Someone. She always remained in the background. She was a "fascinating silence," says Gertrud Von le Fort, a German writer.

Mary was that Mother who silently lost herself in the Son.

The Silence of Virginity

We call her "the Virgin." Virginity in itself is silence and solitude. Although virginity also includes biological and affective aspects, the mystery of virginity embraces a much wider profile.

In the first place, virginity is silence, physiologically and psychologically. The heart of a virgin is essentially a solitary heart. Human emotions of the affective-sexual order, which are of themselves explosive, remain silent; in a virginal heart, everything is calm, in peace, like an extinguished flame. It is not suppressed nor repressed, it is under control.

Virginity has hidden its roots in the mystery of poverty. Possibly, it is the most radical aspect of poverty. I do not understand the contradiction that exists in our post-conciliar period among some of the clergy—the tendency of exalting poverty and underestimating virginity. Could it not be that one party does not understand the other? Could it not be that some clergy want to sail on the crest of a modern fad, exalting "the poor" according to Marxist thought and rejecting virginity according to Freudian thought? Nevertheless, the deep mystery of poverty, just like virginity, unfolds itself on a plane as distant from Marx as it is from Freud...! It does so in the final mystery of God.

Solitude, silence, poverty, virginity—concepts that are so conditioned and intertwined—in themselves are not values, they are empty and void of value. There is only one content that gives them meaning and value: God.

Virginity means full consent to the sovereignty of God, to the full and exclusive presence of the Lord. God himself is the final mystery and the total explanation of virginity.

It is obvious that the psychological constitution of man and woman demand a mutual complementarity. When the true and living God occupies the virginal heart, *vitally and completely,* there is no need of complementarity because the heart is completely occupied and fulfilled. But when God, in fact, does not completely occupy a consecrated heart, then yes, there is a pressing need of "complementarity."

❖

Freudians are totally incapable of understanding the mystery of virginity because they start from a materialistic and atheistic presupposition. They have no authority, they lack a basis for experimentation, and consequently, the "scientific rigor" to understand a "reality" (such as virginity "in" God), which is essentially inaccessible and nonexistent to them.

Virginity without God, without a living and true God, is a human absurdity, from any point of view. Chastity without God is always a repression and leads to neurosis. Let's be clear: if God is not living in a consecrated heart, no normal person in the world could be a virgin or chaste in the radical sense of these words.

Only God is capable of awakening immortal harmonics in the solitary and silent heart of a virgin. The all-powerful God is at the origin of the mystery of our human "liberty." The heart of an authentic virgin is essentially free. A heart consecrated to God in virginity and *truly* inhabited by the divine presence will never permit itself, nor can it permit itself, to be "dependent" on anyone.

This virginal heart can and must love deeply, but it always remains master of itself. This is so because its love is fundamentally a sacrificial and diffusive love. Purely human affection tends to be exclusive and possessive, because it conceals disguised doses of egoism. It is difficult if not impossible to love everyone when we love only one person. Virginal love tends to be sacrificial and universal. It is only from God's perspective that we can expend great energies in favor of our brothers and sisters, energies that have been offered first to God. If virginity does not open its affective tendencies in the service of all, it would be a frustrated existence and, consequently, a false virginity.

Again, this is why virginity must be free. A virginal heart cannot allow itself to be a dominated and absorbed heart, even when it loves and is deeply loved. God is liberty in this heart. Perhaps the unequivocal sign of virginity lies in this: it does not create dependencies nor remain dependent on anyone. The one who is free—the virgin—

always liberates, while loving and being loved. It is God who realizes this equilibrium. Jesus was this way.

If God is the mystery and explanation of virginity, we may conclude that where there is more virginity, there is more plenitude of God and more capacity for loving. Mary is "full of grace," because she is fully virginal. In such wise virginity, in addition to freedom, is plenitude.

Mary is a profound solitude—through her virginity —totally inhabited by her Lord God. God fills her and calms her. The Lord dwells fully in her. He inhabits her completely. This human personality who appears in the Gospels so full of maturity and peace, attentive and obliging to others, is the fruit of a virginity lived to perfection.

An Intimate Scene

The scene of the annunciation (cf. Lk 1:26-38) is a golden narrative. Like a morning dew, this intimacy suffuses persons and movements in the same way that the Spirit of God at the beginning of the world hovered above the formless cosmic mass (cf. Gen 1:2). In this scene the presence of God pulsates, as though we are to witness the eruption of a decisive event in the history of the world.

Gechter, the German exegete, affirms that in the scene of the annunciation one breathes an inimitable and attractive aroma of intimacy.

So as to capture the "breath" of this scene, we must hold our own breath and take a contemplative attitude in attentive quiet. William Ramsay says that when this narrative is read aloud it loses its charm. "It seems to be one of those narratives that loses its enchantment when it is read in public."

We have the impression that it is the angel who presides over the scene. Mary is silent. As usual we feel that she occupies a corner distant from the scene. The young girl observes, reflects and keeps silence.

It is not a pathetic silence. It is the simple attitude depicted in Psalm 123 (v. 2): "As the eyes of a maid are on the hands of her mistress"—attentive and obedient. The angel says everything. Mary expresses only one question and one declaration.

❖

The words shone resplendently like swords (cf. Lk 1:28). Never has anyone else in the world heard such a greeting. What was it? An optical illusion? An internal presence? A spoken discourse or a silent one? Whatever it was, the young girl was declared by heaven to be the privileged one, the enchanted one, the one loved more than any other woman on earth.

Mary "was greatly troubled" (Lk 1:29).

What does this mean? Did she have a breakdown? Was she frightened by the vision and greeting? Did she become agitated by the whole scene, by such a solemn salutation?

It was much deeper than all that. When a person is troubled, her mind confused, she feels unable to coordinate ideas. Here, instead, Luke confirms that Mary, though troubled, began to reflect serenely on the meaning of the words.

Then what did this being "troubled" mean? Equivalent words would be perplexity, confusion. Mary's interior state was like that of a person blushing because, measuring the disproportion between the concept that she has of herself (cf. Lk 1:48) and the majesty of the sublime expressions by which she is being described, she knows herself unworthy of such treatment.

Again, Mary emerges from this scene as one filled with humility, the ultimate root of her greatness.

❖

The apparently imperative expressions of the angel lend themselves to some ambiguity. She was told "you shall conceive," "you shall give him a name," etc. However, in their context, they were not an imposition but a proposition, that is, an assignment which, to be realized, needed Mary's consent.

Once she gives her consent, she enters into a silent passivity, and in an attitude of abandonment she submits herself to the course of the mystery. The Holy Spirit descends upon her like a shadow. "In" her is realized the total Mystery: the "Fruit" germinates "in" her, grows "in" her, is detached from her—in birth—and the name that had been chosen is given to him. All is silence.

Apparently all is passivity. In reality it is fidelity. Mary "is" the unconditional and universal affirmation of the will of the Father. As a servant, she has no will or rights of her own: they belong to her Lord. The initiatives must come from him. On her part, she will execute them faithfully, simply and without dramatization.

❖

This passivity could also be accused of ambiguity. But it is biblical passivity, revolutionary and transforming. If the sapling wishes to be transformed into a slender tree, it must submit to passivity.

If we wish that a piece of bread be transformed into life, an immortal life, it must submit to being passive and permit itself to be attacked and even destroyed by teeth and saliva, by the gastric juices, intestines and liver...until a handful of amino acids is transformed into life, an immortal life.

We will never sufficiently understand that it is much easier to conquer than to be conquered. We will never understand enough that the "here I am" of all the men and women of God in the Bible is the final secret of all spiritual and human greatness and of all fruitfulness.

❖

When the angel retired (cf. Lk 1:38), there was a great silence. What did Mary feel at that moment? Was she dazzled? Perhaps crushed under the weight of such a mystery? In the whole sequence of the apparition, the angel, the words, the assignments...at the summit of the exaltation, what did Mary feel? Dizziness? Fright? Surprise? Joy?

If we remember the normal reactions of Mary and her spirituality of the poor of Yahweh, we can conclude that before all of this splendor Mary must have said: "Here I am. What are you expecting from me? I am willing, Father."

But in spite of that humble disposition of Mary, the angel saw that he had imposed an almost insupportable weight on the shoulders of the young girl. Although immaculate in her conception and highly privileged, she still remained a creature like us, subject to psychological reactions such as fear and confusion.

With the passing of time the freshness of this extraordinary experience could fade away; the first symptoms of her pregnancy would begin to be felt. The young woman would feel drawn into complete solitude and silence, like the victim of some hallucination. Her composure could crumble under the poundings of discouragement and she could find herself sailing between the brilliant lights of the past and the obscure shadows of the present.

If such a situation should arise, where would the poor creature find something to cling to? The angel understood this possible event and he stretched forth his hand to Mary and deposited into her hands something to hold on to: he offered her a parallel occurrence with which she could compare her own case.

"Look at your relative, Elizabeth," said the angel. "She was sterile yet now she is in her sixth month of pregnancy. Everyone says 'the sterile one is flourishing' because for God nothing is impossible. You yourself can verify if all this is true. And that will serve as a proof that all I have just announced to you is and will be a reality."

Was this so? A solid anchor to save her from shipwreck in the sea of solitude? Was it a "sign" to secure her faith? It seems so from the context of the annunciation. It was a delicate gesture on the part of the angel. In spite of the spiritual fortitude of Mary, there always exists a margin of psychological frailty in human beings. And God is so understanding!

But from what we already know of Mary during her whole life, I would say that the breadth of Mary's faith was such that she did not need that kind of help or proof. It was sufficient that she be told that nothing is impossible for God (cf. Lk 1:37). One who belongs to the *poor of Yahweh* does not ask, nor question, nor doubt, nor complain. She surrenders. Explanations and proofs are superfluous.

CHAPTER 8

A Dramatic Silence

The Well-guarded Secret

After the annunciation the silence of Mary is very moving. That she became the Mother of the Messiah and that it was done miraculously were sufficient to cause a nervous breakdown in anyone.

It is difficult to bear such a psychological weight alone and in silence. If Mary kept this secret in complete silence then we stand before a unique case of human greatness, the circumstances of which are worth analyzing carefully.

Mary did not tell anyone the secret of the virginal Incarnation.

She did not tell Joseph (cf. Mt 1:19).

She did not tell Elizabeth. When Mary arrived at Zechariah's home in Ain Karim, Elizabeth already knew the secret, at least in its broad outlines; as for the details, we do not know. Scarcely had Mary opened her lips to say "shalom," when Elizabeth burst into exclamations and congratulations. Possibly the same angel who had told the secret of Elizabeth's pregnancy to Mary (cf. Lk 1:36) had told Mary's secret to Elizabeth.

The Nazareans did not know when Jesus was conceived. Had they known, their slander would have followed Mary without ceasing, and the Child would have suffered from it more than the Mother.

When Jesus presented himself in the synagogue of Nazareth declaring that he was the awaited Messiah, the Nazareans "took offense at him" (Mk 6:3). Luke adds that they pursued him as if chasing a dog, with stones in their hands, leading him to the brow of a hill to hurl him down headlong and kill him (cf. Lk 4:28-30). The Gospel of Matthew recalls that the Nazareans, on that same occasion, said all they could to humiliate Jesus, claiming that he was no better than they were; that he was simply the son of a carpenter and a carpenter himself; that his mother was a poor villager; that he had never studied and was ignorant of the Scriptures; and finally, "here we all know one another..." (cf. Mt 13:53-58).

This is how these poor people unleashed their bad feelings about Jesus so as to diminish his prestige. This is all they knew. Had they suspected even vaguely that Jesus was not the proper son of Joseph, then on this occasion with what glee they would have used the most derogatory word of their popular slang: "son of a raped woman" *("harufa")!*

❖

From the gospel context we can conclude therefore that Mary did not share her secret with anyone, not even with her own mother. If she had done so, it is most likely that her mother would have talked about it to a sister in whom she trusted, but then, after some time, the secret would have filtered down to the market place. And all the more in a small town where everyone knew the background on everyone else....

These people, like Simeon and Anna who were inspired by the Holy Spirit and spoke prophetically about the future of Jesus and Mary, had no idea about the virginal conception, as we can deduce from the context. On the other hand, in public opinion and in the Gospels Jesus always appears as the son of a normal marriage.

All of this therefore indicates that the secret did not leave the lips of Mary. She hid herself with her own secret, in the silence of her heart. She broke away from public opinion, she disregarded what people might say, she abandoned herself to the will of the Father and remained in peace.

Inner Strength

Any woman in Israel would have been ecstatic had she experienced what Mary encountered in the annunciation.

Since the time of Abraham, but more so after the royalty had been established in the land, millions of Jewish women had harbored one golden dream: to be mother of the Messiah.

In addition, a popular legend was kept alive in Israel according to which every woman who gave birth to a son would have an indirect share in the glory of the future Messiah. In other words every Jewish mother would participate in the motherhood of the Messiah, even if it came centuries in the future.

As a consequence of this popular myth there arose in Israel a radical scorn toward virginity and a great fear of sterility, because both were obstacles to a woman's sharing in the glory of the Messiah. Thus the greatest frustration for a woman was to become a spinster, and the greatest humiliation was to be sterile. The shame of barren women such as Sarah, Hannah, Elizabeth, and the daughter of Jephthah, who "mourned her virginity on the mountains" of Israel (Jgs 11:38), gives just an echo of that popular legend.

At the moment of the annunciation it was announced to Mary that this fantastic dream harbored by so many women in Israel would be realized precisely in her. And what is more, it would happen in a miraculous manner through the exceptional intervention of God himself. Mary, a thoughtful and informed woman, was conscious of the far-reaching effects of what was offered to her.

Now if a woman in such circumstances is still able to control her emotions and remain in complete silence, she must possess an outstanding maturity.

Without this maturity, an ordinary woman would feel incapable of handling such incredible news. Her nerves would betray her, she would experience a torrent of emotions, she would give vent to her feelings, weep, tell someone, fall apart. If Mary is able to keep silent without telling anything to anyone, accepting completely the weight of this enormous secret, then she is certainly a lady in full command of herself.

❖

Let us then investigate the psychological reason, apart from grace, for this interior strength of Mary.

In the first place Mary was a contemplative woman and as all contemplatives she possessed a great maturity. The contemplative is one who is selfless. She is, to be precise, an admiring soul, ever grateful. She has a great capacity for being amazed.[1]

She is an enraptured person, stirred by Someone. Hence she is never all to herself or self-centered; she is always in a state of "exodus," of going out to the Other. Living in the contemplative there is always a You, an Other.

Psychiatry tells us that the capacity for amazement is in complete opposition to narcissism. If the contemplative is always turned to the Other without any reference to herself, she has no measure of narcissism. In this person there is no infantilism—narcissism and infantilism are the same—she is fully mature, her reactions are marked by objectivity and wisdom. She will not be carried away by success nor depressed by defeat. She will not be dominated but self-mastered.

❖

Mary, being an authentic contemplative, has this interior strength. We have only to analyze the "Magnificat." *All of Mary* is a vibrating harp touched by the Lord. In this canticle she does not refer to herself. Only incidentally does she speak of herself, and it is to say that she is "lowly."

The canticle of Mary is in the same vein as Psalm 8: "O LORD, our Lord, how glorious is your name over all the earth!" (v. 2) It brings out the same overtones as Paul's exclamation: "Oh, the depth of the riches and wisdom and knowledge of God! How inscrutable are his judgments and how unsearchable his ways!" (Rom 11:33) The "Magnificat" can be summarized thus: "Elizabeth, how magnificent is our God!"

> You have done great things;
> O God, who is like you?

> *—Psalm 71:19*

To a woman like Mary, with such a capacity for grateful wonder, "her" things do not have any importance, only the things of God do. She lives detached from her own interests. Her interior world cannot be touched or moved by news relating to herself. She is beyond all that and above emotional fluctuations.

Adversities do not depress her nor does she exult because of good news. Such is the immovable stability of Mary's soul.

The Circle Closes

To attain knowledge of the person and life of Mary it is imperative that we place ourselves in the cultural and religious milieu in which Mary lived and remember the customs of Palestine of that period. What we today call Palestine then comprised Judea, Samaria and Galilee, that is, all of Israel. As the Gospels speak so little of Mary, so too their historical perspective is full of gaps.

In order to cover these voids we will adopt a golden rule: whatever was common and normal in her times and in her village, was common and normal for Mary.

❖

Until the age of twelve and a day, Mary was considered, like all others, a "child." At twelve and a day she was declared *gedulah,* which means an adult, hence marriageable. The law supposed that she had acquired physical and psychological maturity. Very soon after she had attained the age of twelve, according to the customs of that time, the father of the family handed over his daughter "in espousals."[2]

Luke says that God sent the angel Gabriel "to a virgin betrothed to a man named Joseph" (Lk 1:27).

Therefore, Mary was "betrothed" but not married. After the ceremony of the "espousals," the young girl remained promised, engaged but not married. We would say today that she was a fiancée. There was an interval of some twelve months between the "espousals" and the marriage itself which was called the "nuptial procession," because then the fiancée was led solemnly into the house of her husband-to-be.

During these months, like all the other "promised ones," Mary remained in the house of her father. The latter determined and prepared the trousseau, the dowry, the date of the wedding, and also the money that the groom would have to bring to the matrimony. The father exercised over the "betrothed" full paternal authority.

Nevertheless, in spite of the fact that the two "betrothed" did not live together till the day of the marriage "procession," the "espousals" began what we could call a true juridical bond between the two that was in a certain sense equivalent to marriage, so much so that the law considered the groom *baealah*, "lord" of the bride.

❖

During the months of the "espousals," the bride guarded her virginity most carefully. In fact, according to the customs of Galilee (this detail comes from the historian Flavius Josephus) during these months the fiancées were not allowed to be alone with one another. On the day of the "procession," two women were designated to examine the bride to ascertain that she was still a virgin. If it was proven that she had lost her virginity, a curse fell upon her, and she was called *harufa*, a crude expression used to indicate that she had been raped.

If it could be proven that she had had intercourse with a man other than her bridegroom, she was then considered to be adulterous along with all its consequences and the groom, who was considered her "lord," could and normally did serve her a decree of divorce.

According to Leviticus, she could be stoned to death in the public square. Again, according to information from Flavius Josephus, if the girl happened to be the daughter of a Levite, she could be burned alive.

We need to place ourselves in the context of these customs so as to appreciate in all its dimensions the value of Mary's silence while she was pregnant during the pre-marriage days.

The circle is now complete.

Hanging over an Abyss

It was during the time of these "espousals" that Mary was told that she was to conceive by the Holy Spirit. And before living together with Joseph she found herself pregnant. Thus Mary was hanging over an abyss.

> This supernatural mystery led her into the most delicate of circumstances. Being only promised, conception came in a period which excluded all conjugal relationships, according to the mind of true Israelites.[3]

Here the drama of Mary's silence begins. With the passing of months the visible consequences of the Incarnation would become more and more evident. This fact could give rise to rumors of all sorts, including adultery. She could be stoned in the public square according to custom and the law. Humanly speaking, she was lost.

What was she to do? Explain what had happened to some relatives so that they would transmit this to public opinion? Nobody would believe it. Besides, the explanation was as absurd as it was childish; Mary would be the object of general ridicule and the rumor would spread like wild fire. Worst of all, the echoes of the curse would one day fall upon the Son.

What should she do? Consult a person of complete trust? She did not do it. She remained quiet, abandoned into the hands of the Father. To know what really happened, we must have recourse to what I would call a mystical explanation. Anyone who has had a vivid experience of God will understand what we have to say.

❖

When a person lives intensely in the presence of God, when a soul experiences truly and vitally that God is the infinite treasure, the most loving Father, that he is all good and the supreme Good, that he is sweetness, patience, and fortitude, the human being can experience such vitality, such plenitude, such joy and delight that, at that moment, all things on earth seem insignificant next to God. After tasting the love of the Father, all things in comparison are worthless, secondary. Prestige? Smoke and ashes.

God is such a wonder that the one who experiences him feels totally free. The "I" is taken up by the "You," fears disappear, everything is secure and one finds oneself invulnerable although facing an entire army (cf. Ps 27). Neither life, nor death, nor persecution, nor sickness, nor calumny, nor lies, nothing will make me tremble if my Father is with me (cf. Rom 8:38).

This is exactly what happened to Mary.

❖

As explained in the chapter on her motherhood, during the time of pregnancy Mary was "inhabited" by the Word and the Holy Spirit *in person;* the intertrinitarian operations were circumscribed in the somatic or bodily confines of Mary. The presence of God in her was unique. We see in the "Magnificat" that Mary was going through an extraordinary experience of God. Her soul "exulted," mad with joy for her God.

During these months Mary must have experienced, with an insurmountable intensity, that the Lord God is gentleness and tenderness, mercy and love, that the Father is a most brilliant emerald, plenitude so inexpressible that words will never describe it, the mind never conceive it, the heart never dream of it, that all the rest in comparison has neither value nor importance.

Mary felt an immense sensation of freedom; she felt tremendously secure, and even invulnerable before any adversity, capable of exclaiming with the psalmist: "Blessed be the LORD whose wondrous kindness he has shown me in a fortified city" (Ps 31:22).

> The LORD is with me; I fear not;
> what can man do against me?
>
> —*Psalm 118:6*

It is as if she said: "God is my treasure and my only good, they can do with me what they want. A curse? Stoning? Isolation? A libel of repudiation? Nothing has any importance. God alone is my treasure. Only God is important. The rest is dust."

And Mary remained in silence. She felt immensely free.

The Just Man

We understand and admire Mary for guarding her secret silently. But why did she not tell Joseph? The fact of the conception by the Holy Spirit and its consequences were of utmost interest to Joseph. From the time of the "espousals" Joseph was "her lord"; juridically speaking Mary belonged to Joseph. Why did she not tell him? This is certainly very strange.

Events unfolded in this way: one day the news reached Joseph—how, we do not know—that Mary was pregnant. Not wishing to cause a public scandal against Mary, he decided to present her secretly with an act of divorce. He had just begun the formalities in that regard (cf. Mt 1:18-25), when God unveiled the mystery.

In the background of these events some half-hidden aspects are revealed which ennoble both Mary and Joseph.

❖

To judge the reaction of Joseph and his behavior in this scene we must remind ourselves of certain elements of common psychology. In the face of public opinion one of the greatest humiliations for a married man is the fact or rumor that his wife has been unfaithful. In such a circumstance the normal reaction of a man is ordinarily of a violent nature. Immediately revolvers and daggers flash in the sun. A human way of saving one's honor, as it is commonly said.

If it has always been so, we can imagine what it would have been like in a patriarchal society such as that in which Joseph lived. It is enough to open the book of Leviticus. We know what awaited adulterers: automatic divorce, a great scandal, a rain of stones.

Why didn't Joseph react this way? In view of this event we can guess some interesting conclusions. In the first chapter of Matthew we see Joseph perplexed, as though he could not believe what he had heard or seen. This allows us to draw the following conclusion.

❖

I think that Mary's being immaculate and full of grace must have been reflected in her face, in all her reactions and in her general comportment. Mary must have had, since her childhood, something very special about her. That young girl would have radiated, it seems to me, something divine, surrounding her body and personality with a mysterious aura, at least to a sensitive observer.

From the reaction of Joseph we can presuppose that before the events we are analyzing he must have felt something toward Mary like admiration, perhaps even veneration. Matthew presents Joseph as being "just," that is, *sensitive to the things of God.* Joseph, therefore, must have seen in Mary more than an attractive young girl; he must have sensed in her something special, something different, a mystery.

Thus we explain the reaction of Joseph. It seems that, confronting the "rumor" with the idea that he had of her, he was perplexed and could only say: "It cannot be." It was impossible that the angelic creature whom he knew perfectly could have stumbled that way. But, on the other hand, there was the evidence. What was it all about? What should he do?

His esteem for Mary was so high that he decided, whatever had happened, not to give way to the typical violence of the betrayed husband, but to suffer in silence this whole situation, eventually leaving Nazareth, as long as Mary was not mistreated by public opinion.

All of this expresses the great veneration Joseph felt toward Mary and how venerable Mary must have been from childhood. At the same time this reaction shows us in one event the whole character of Joseph: sensitive to the things of God, worrying more about others than himself, full of understanding and forgiveness, capable restraining himself from making a hasty decision, capable of trusting and prefering to suffer himself rather than have others suffer, capable of loving unconditionally.

A Reverent Seal

In spite of all that has been said, we are still haunted by the question: Why did Mary not communicate to Joseph a fact that concerned him so directly?

Mary must have clearly understood that sooner or later Joseph would be informed, and the later he found out the worse it would be for her. Why did she keep silent? Did she think that Joseph would not be able to understand such a deep mystery? In reality, who could? Hence, was it not better for her to remain silent? Did Mary wonder if Joseph would not believe in the objective presentation of the facts? Actually, this event was so unparalleled that anyone would think that under the cloak of a childish excuse Mary was hiding her own blunder. Would it be that? A calculated silence?

❖

It was not a tactic. I suspect it was rather a seal of deep respect in the presence of a tremendous mystery. Because here we find the real answer to this awkward silence. Mary remained overwhelmed and profoundly moved by the mystery of the Incarnation.

We already know that she was an intelligent and thoughtful person. She gauged the importance and transcendence of the double prodigy: the motherhood of God and a virginal maternity. She who was so humble and thought herself to be so "lowly" (cf. Lk 1:48), felt that she was unworthy of all this, and she concluded that the best way to be thankful for and faithful to such gratuity was to reverence this whole mystery by a complete silence.

This was all so unique and sacred that it appeared to her that to share it with a human being, even someone like Joseph, would be a profanation.

Thus, since she refused to reveal the most sacred secret of history in order to be faithful to her God with her silence, Mary was disposed to suffer any consequence: the popular curse, the act of divorce, stones, flames, social rejection and human solitude. Anything.

Yes, all that came from God was so great and what came from human beings so small! God was for her the reward, the inheritance, the gift, the wealth! She had been treated with such predilection that all the rest was worthless.

The Mother remained in silence, unconcerned, tranquil. God is great!

❖

And the Lord, moved by the silent fidelity of his daughter, came to her assistance.

With an extraordinary divine intervention, God had placed her in a blind alley. The only one who could save her from this predicament was God himself. This he did by means of another extraordinary intervention.

An interior revelation, clear as daylight, came to Joseph: "Joseph, leave aside all fears. Mary is not a woman of the street. She is the one chosen among women of all times. The Lord has cast his eyes upon her and found her most pleasing. Mary has committed no shameful act. What has germinated in her is the direct and exceptional operation of the Holy Spirit. Joseph, take her willingly to your home and keep her as the living sanctuary of the living God" (cf. Mt 1:20-24).

❖

From that moment on Joseph could not but approach Mary with an infinite reverence. If, according to the context of Matthew's first chapter, Joseph had an inkling that Mary was different from others, this revelation must have confirmed his profound appreciation for her.

Because of this revelation, Joseph's respect for Mary increased. A man sensitive to the things of God, Joseph must have regarded her with an attitude filled with reverence, affection and admiration. In a man who had been "touched" by God so deeply, the affective and merely human bonds of love were transformed and elevated. To Joseph she was more than an attractive young girl. She was the revered shrine of the living God.

According to the opinion of many, myself included, it was from that moment that Mary and Joseph decided mutually to live a virginal life in the matrimonial state.

Between them they would take care of and protect Jesus, the direct fruit of God, germinated in the solitary womb of his holy Mother. God had chosen that house and that marriage as a very special dwelling, holier than the ancient Ark of the Covenant. It was worth overcoming the laws of the flesh and living in a state of adoration.

❖

Joseph's reaction to the angel's revelation is most interesting. Verse 24 of Matthew's first chapter gives the impression that Joseph immediately took the initiative. He rapidly made preparations for the nuptial "procession" and, in a solemn ceremony, took Mary as his wife.

God had entrusted to him the care of Mary and the Child. The first thing to do was to make sure that a malicious rumor against the Mother, and later against the Child, would not be set aflame, since the first symptoms of pregnancy were beginning to show. Hence his haste.

Joseph appears here a gentleman of great prudence.

CHAPTER 9

A Miracle in the Midst of Silence

Friendship and Communion

In true life with God, immersion in intimacy with him is accompanied by and brings about self-giving service to others. The more intense the encounter with God, the more extensive will openness to others be.

The experience of God which does not lead to communion with others is simply a subtle evasion in which one seeks oneself. There must be a perpetual interchange between life with God and fellowship with others. They must be integrated and grow together, without dichotomy.

Mary lived an unparalleled intimacy with God. That intimacy would bring her to a unprecedented communion with others, represented in this case by Elizabeth. God is like that. The true God is One who never leaves us in peace, but always leads us to peace. The Lord is always uprooting his friends to lead them to an encounter with their brothers and sisters.

Mary, after living through the great emotions of the annunciation, did not linger, savoring the banquet. On the contrary, the energy born of her contact with the Lord gave her wings to fly across "the hill country in haste to a town of Judah" (Lk 1:39) to the house of Elizabeth.

God himself united them. The Lord had revealed to Elizabeth what had happened to Mary, at least in essence, if not in detail. And the same Lord revealed to Mary what had happened to Elizabeth (cf. Lk 1:36).

Both felt deeply moved and grateful for having been, to different degrees, an object of predilection on the part of the Most High.

Elizabeth did not leave the house during the first five months of her pregnancy (cf. Lk 1:24). Why? To avoid being seen? She herself said "the Lord...has seen fit to take away my disgrace before others" (Lk 1:25). Hence, she considered her pregnancy a cause for holy pride.

It is also possible that Elizabeth was deeply impressed by the extraordinary action of the Almighty who, in an exceptional way, had intervened in nature and in history through her. During the first months she remained hidden in her home, in silence and in prayer, surely in order to live intensely the generosity of the Lord.

Elizabeth's own words reflect this impression when Luke writes: "and she went into seclusion for five months, saying, 'So has the Lord done for me...'" (Lk 1:24-25).

❖

Apparently Mary prepared her trip with some urgency and the traveling itself was somewhat hasty. Why such urgency? To verify the pregnancy of Elizabeth and thus confirm for herself the veracity of the annunciation? To unburden herself, speaking about the great secret, since Elizabeth was the only one who knew? Perhaps to find an advocate, suspects Gechter, in case she should be accused of adultery?

Whatever the reason, Luke's words, "During those

days Mary set out and traveled to the hill country in haste" (Lk 1:39), show that Mary's journey took place not long after the annunciation. This means that the interval between the annunciation and the visitation must have been brief.

Nevertheless, it would be naive to think that Mary left immediately for the mountain region of Judah. She needed the consent of her father, under whom she was still a dependent. She also needed the permission of Joseph, her "lord" since the time of the espousals.

How did she obtain these authorizations? Her situation was quite delicate. How could she avoid disclosing the real reason for the trip—unveiling the mystery of the virginal Incarnation—and at the same time offer a convincing explanation for the journey? Through a mental reservation? Let us not forget that although Mary was very young she possessed a basic maturity, balance and wisdom.

Mary must have combined truth and wisdom, arriving at a satisfactory explanation toward obtaining permission for her trip. All of this shows that Mary was confronted with the same kinds of problems and difficulties that we face.

❖

She could not travel alone. She had to join a party or caravan. She had to cross Galilee, Samaria and part of Judea. On her passage through Judea, in the last section of the road which runs westward from Jericho to Jerusalem, she would come across the area described in the parable of the good Samaritan (cf. Lk 10:30-37).

The fact that she traveled "in haste" did not refer, according to Gechter, to a kind of nervousness or anxiety to share the secret or to confirm what the angel had told her.

It meant rather that the journey must have been made with very few stops and without entering Jerusalem.

Tradition locates the house of Zechariah in a place called Ain Karim, about three and a half miles west of Jerusalem. On arriving there Mary greeted Elizabeth (cf. Lk 1:40). How strange! She entered Zechariah's house and greeted *Elizabeth!* Among the Jews, it was the man who held all authority and responsibility and much more so when, as in this case, he was a priest. Against all protocol, there, in the center of the scene, the Holy Spirit compelled Elizabeth to speak prophetic words (cf. Lk 1:41-43). God himself spoke through Elizabeth.

❖

Elizabeth was a woman "advanced in years" (Lk 1:7). The context of Luke's Gospel implies that Elizabeth had long since passed the age of bearing children.

> We must suppose that Elizabeth was in her sixties when she became pregnant. If Mary was the first-born in her family, Mary's mother must have been, according to normal calculations, about twenty-eight years old, perhaps more, if Mary had older brothers or sisters.[4]

It was, then, impossible for Elizabeth to be a cousin of Mary, as is commonly said. Mary would have been between twelve and fifteen years old at this time. Thus Elizabeth must have been her aunt, even her great-aunt. But this is not important.

It is very strange that two women so distant in age were so close in their hearts. There was something that both could share in, beyond distance and age. How is it that they became so intimate with one another? The family bond? Such intimacy is not always present between relatives.

How can we explain this? We may put forward a few hypotheses. First, perhaps since John the Baptist and Jesus had to be united in their destinies and in their lives, the Holy Spirit arranged that their mothers would likewise be united in a special communion. This would also mean that both mothers had a decisive influence in the formation and spirituality of their sons.

There is another hypothesis. In the Gospel, Elizabeth appears as a woman of great interior sensitivity, like those women who possess a penetrating intuition in accurately detecting any spiritual movement. And Mary, as we have explained, by her Immaculate Conception and her predestination in becoming the Mother of God, must have had a special aura about her since her earliest years.

It is probable, then, that from the time Mary was a child, Elizabeth detected in her a privileged soul—because of the depth and early maturity of her spiritual life. Perhaps Elizabeth foresaw in Mary, though still obscurely, an exalted destiny, perhaps the original purity of her conception, or at least an exceptional interior richness.

Given this latter supposition, there must have been an earlier exchange of intimacies, of personal experiences in the "things" of God between the two women, in spite of the difference in age.

❖

In the Lukan scene (cf. Lk 1:39-56), Mary listens and reflects. She does not speak. When she does break the silence, it is to express her emotions and sing to her Lord. Her words, more than a song, are an exaltation. From the "Magnificat" we can conclude that as with all great contemplatives, God awakened in Mary an indescribable jubilation. This is valid evidence to confirm our conviction that Mary not only belongs to the line of contemplatives, but that she is the crown and model of them all.

Mary stayed with Elizabeth for almost three months (cf. Lk 1:56). What did the two of them talk about during those three months? What were the essence and central focus of their conversations?

In my opinion, the "Magnificat," (perhaps also the "Benedictus" of Zechariah), reflects the nature of the conversations and exchanges of impressions between Elizabeth and Mary.

They spoke about the consolation of Israel, of the promises made to our fathers, of the mercy poured out from generation to generation from the time of Abraham until our days, of the exaltation of the poor and the fall of the powerful.

But more than talking about the poor, the prophets, and the chosen, they spoke about the Lord himself, about Yahweh God. When one feels intensely loved by the Father, one cannot help but speak about him. Mary, recalling that she was the center of all privileges, from the Immaculate Conception to the virginal motherhood, would feel a special desire to speak about her God and Father. Resch affirms: "Never could we find a higher expression of the sublime feelings that Mary must have experienced at this moment."

All the emotions that overflowed from these two exceptional women and which they shared together are reflected in the "Magnificat." It is nothing less than a spiritual proclamation and a summary of the impressions and interior experiences of both women.

God, God himself, was the basis and the object of their emotions, their conversations and their growth during those three months in Ain Karim.

All the exegetes agree that from the first two chapters of Luke a feminine figure emerges with a very specific profile: delicate, devoted and silent.

For this reason, Harnack found it "surprising" that Mary would interrupt her habitual silence and intimacy with such an exalted canticle. To this objection Gechter responds with a very plausible psychological explanation:

> Her deep piety was swept up by the greatness of what God had done in her.
>
> More could not be expected for the silent character of the Virgin than that she would burst aloud in a joyful outpouring of words.
>
> This being an exceptional occasion, there is nothing which contradicts her habitual reserve and modesty.[5]

Naturally, it was not only a spiritual effusion and a deep fellowship. It was more than that. There was also a fraternal solicitude and assistance.

The angel had told Mary that Elizabeth was in her sixth month. A short time after this Mary went to Elizabeth's house, and the evangelist adds, "Mary remained with her about three months" (Lk 1:56). From these details we can conclude that Mary must have stayed in Ain Karim until after Elizabeth gave birth.

Mary emerges from this picture a delicate young lady with a deep spirit of fraternal availability. It is easy to imagine the situation. Elizabeth is in a state of imminent childbirth with possible complications due to her advanced age, almost useless as regards domestic chores. Zechariah was dumb, "wounded" psychologically. No doubt the two lived alone. For them Mary was a blessing sent from heaven.

We can imagine Mary just as she always appears—attentive and caring. We can picture her busy with all the ordinary daily chores: cooking, cleaning, washing, weaving cloth; preparing all that was needed for the baby; helping Elizabeth in the delicate prenatal care, serving first as a nurse and after as a midwife; consoling Zechariah by insisting on the mercy of the Lord; always preoccupied with the thousand details of a home....

She was kindness personified.

Why Did She Marry?

A few decades ago, the scholar Paul Gechter created an intense polemic with his exegetical interpretation of Luke 1:34. This author claimed that Mary, with her words "I do not know man," was not alluding to a vow of virginity, but simply referring to her actual juridical situation.

It is as though she had said: "Angel Gabriel, how could I be pregnant now if, during this period of espousals, I am not living, nor can live, with Joseph until the day of the 'procession'"? According to Gechter, these words did not have a bearing on the past or on the future, as if she would say: "I have not known, nor do I know, nor do I intend to know a man." Rather, the words "I do not know" had to be understood rigorously in the present tense.

Another noted German scholar, Josef Schmid,[6] shared the same opinion, saying that these words refer to the fact that "at that moment she was only promised and not married," and that "the expression of a vow, or at least a firm decision of perpetual virginity" cannot be understood from these words.

However, Catholic tradition, following the interpretation of St. Augustine, has given the verb "I do not know" in the present tense a fullness which embraces the past, the present and the future, as though it were an impersonal verb which embraced all tenses of the verb conjugation.

It is as though she said: "I do not intend to have conjugal relations with any man during my whole life." All languages, says Ricciotti, an Italian scholar, including modern languages, use the conjugation of a verb in the present tense with an extended view to the future, as when we say: "I do not study medicine; I do not go to foreign countries; I am not marrying this woman...." It is in this sense that Mary spoke in Luke 1:34.

We must distinguish two realities: the virginal birth and perpetual virginity.

The virgin birth is a given fact, proven in many ways in the Gospels, and from the point of view of faith it is an unquestionable fact. Those who deny it are those who do not admit miracles as a principle to begin with.

Perpetual virginity has biblical foundations, but its principal strength comes from Tradition. It is a dogmatic doctrine defined at the Lateran Council in the year 649. In any case, perpetual virginity is one of the most solid foundations of mariology, and one of the most solid and ancient teachings of the Church.

It is beyond the scope of the present book to enter into a critical study on so vast a subject. Here, the value and meaning of virginity is what will be discussed.

❖

In my opinion, the strongest argument in favor of Mary's perpetual virginity is rooted, though indirectly, in the fact that Jesus, before dying, entrusted his Mother to the care of John.

If Mary had had more sons, it would have been absurd both from the affective and the juridical point of view to entrust her to the care of a stranger, establishing, besides, a mother-son relationship with him (John). In spite of the fact that this episode (cf. Jn 19:25-28) also embraces a messianic significance, as we shall amply explain later, it does not exclude on the part of Jesus an intended family responsibility. Thus it was interpreted by John, since he "took her into his home" (Jn 19:27).

For me, this fact is an incontrovertible though indirect proof for Mary's perpetual virginity. It seems to me biblically it is the strongest argument. At the death of Jesus, an only son, Mary was left alone without any direct relative. Jesus entrusted her to John's loving care until the end of her life.

❖

What then can be said about the vow of perpetual virginity? There is a growing consensus among mariologists that the decision to live virginally was conceived, decided upon and formulated by Mary after the annunciation. This intuition seems to me most compatible with what we know of Mary's personality.

As we already know, Mary was a thoughtful and deeply spiritual woman. She must have been greatly impressed at how much God appreciated virginity, contrary to all public opinion throughout the history of Israel, and at how he definitively associated virginity with the mystery of the Incarnation.

According to her custom Mary must have turned over and over in her mind this "novelty" which caused a real impasse for her. With the light and presence of the Holy Spirit, she realized that no woman had ever become pregnant without the involvement of a man; that for God everything is possible. She had been chosen precisely for the realization of this prodigious maternity while remaining a virgin. Deeply touched and grateful for such a mission, she must have progressively come to the conclusion that she could pay homage to the Lord by remaining a virgin forever. If the person of the Son of God was to fill her womb, it would not be fitting that any other should do so. Her body would be for God alone.

Why did she marry? With the annunciation all her plans had been changed. She had been taken and thrown into a whirlwind of events that placed her in a most singular situation.

Before the annunciation, as Schmid explains,[7] Mary was destined to be married, in an ordinary marriage. But now, after these events, since her destiny was exceptional, she also had to live in an exceptional situation.

Why did she marry? If Mary had a son without being married, an untenable situation would result for her, and more so for the Son.

It is easy to imagine the situation: in a small town where the human universe is very limited, where everyone knows the "story" of everyone else—magnified, of course, where people live on prejudices and customs, where privacy is almost nonexistent because everything is in full view, easy and tasty morsels for evil tongues—it is easy to imagine that Mary's situation as an unmarried mother would be intolerable. And worse, it would be impossible for Jesus to later exercise any evangelizing activity.

❖

As we said above, it must have been with the utmost respect that Joseph drew near to Mary, after the Lord had revealed to him her destiny and dignity.

And both, so sensitive to the things of God, after long conversations, would have come to the compromise of living united in a virginal matrimony, thus giving cover to the sacrosanct mystery of the Incarnation and cooperating with Jesus Christ in the salvation of the world.

A modern reader understands this with difficulty because of the secularized and Freudian atmosphere in which we live. To understand it, we need to enter into the world of two persons for whom the only reality and value was God.

The Miracle and Its Climax

As the angel departed, the miracle began. The Holy Spirit, bearer of the creative power of the Father, came down and occupied Mary's entire universe. What was it like? What happened during the first minute? The first hour? The first day?

On the day of Pentecost, the Holy Spirit flashed like tongues of fire and shook the earth, manifesting the power of his *effects* rather than his "personal" presence. Now, for Mary, it was a "personal" descent. How was this done? What happened? Was it an emotional trembling, perhaps physical? Did Mary fall unconscious, as though she was paralyzed or possessed by a strange, superhuman power? Was she given extraordinary gifts, spectacular signs? What did she feel during the first days, the first hours?

❖

As we do not possess any biblical indications regarding this, we will have recourse to two points of departure: the style of God and the style of Mary.

As to God's normal operations, we know that from all eternity he was silent. God lives in the depths of souls, in silence. He acts in the universe and in history as one who is unknown. For some, he sleeps; for others, he is dead; for still others, he is nothing. God prefers the night; he loves peace. The Bible says that he is not present in the hurricane (cf. 1 Kgs 19:11).

As for Mary, we already know her attitudes: always reserved, in the background, humble, modest.

A combination of these two styles would give us an idea of what happened that day: the world did not wait in suspense, universal order was not upset, history did not hold its breath. On the contrary, everything happened *naturally, silently.* Never as then did the solemn words of the book of Wisdom ring so true:

> For when peaceful stillness compassed everything
> and the night in its swift course was half spent,
> Your all-powerful word from heaven's royal throne
> bounded...into the doomed land...."
>
> —Wisdom 18:14-15

The evangelical context, analyzed in different parts of this book, indicates that nothing extraordinary had been detected in Mary by the Nazareans, by her close relatives, or even by her parents. The great mystery did not make itself obvious.

Just as virginity is silence and solitude, so in the silent womb of a solitary virgin, without fanfare and without ostentation, the miracle took place.

Now, if exteriorly there were no manifestations, there must have been great changes within Mary's heart. Mary's interior life must have been exceedingly illumined and enriched. She must have been flooded with an avalanche of graces and consolations.

Perhaps her appearance also changed. In what sense? She always appeared deeply recollected. Now she must have looked more so, wishing to live with a new intensity that unique presence of the Spirit and of the Eternal Word.

❖

During these nine months, Mary lived something unique and never to be repeated: a symbiotic identification and intimacy with the One who was silently developing within her.

As we know, between a pregnant mother and the child in her womb the phenomenon of symbiosis occurs. This means that two lives constitute only one life. The baby breathes by means of the mother and with her. Through the umbilical cord, the infant is fed by the mother and through her. In a word, there are two persons with one life, or one life in two persons.

Naturally, Mary did not know the physiology. But an intelligent mother like Mary intuits, and above all, *lives* this symbiotic reality.

Being also a deeply devout woman, this phenomenon must have caused an indescribable sensation in Mary, in the following sense: the creature (Mary) *depended* on the Creator so much so that if the Creator withdrew his creative hand, the creature, Mary, would return to nothingness. At the same time, the Creator depended on the creature, Mary, so that if the creature stopped feeding the Baby, the life of the Creator would be in danger. Such a phenomenon never existed before and will never happen again.

❖

Symbiosis is a physiological phenomenon. The same phenomenon, when it occurs in psychology, is called "intimacy."

Every person, as an experiencing and psychological reality, leads a spiritual life. Now, when two spiritual lives are intertwined and cast into one another, an intimacy—a spiritual symbiosis—is created through which the two persons form only one presence.

Mary experienced simultaneously a physiological symbiosis and a spiritual intimacy. What must that have been! Neither the most penetrating feminine intuition nor the most vivid imagination could ever delve into the height and the depth, the vastness and the intensity of Mary's life during those nine months.

During the long nights, in her sleep or sleeplessness, during her walks to the spring or on the hill, in the synagogue or during the ritual prayers demanded by the Torah, when she was working in the garden or taking care of the flock on the hill, when she was weaving wool or kneading bread...Mary, prostrated interiorly, submissive, full of the Lord, concentrating on and penetrated by that presence, identified herself with the One who was the life of her life, the soul of her soul.... Never in the history of the world has any woman lived such vital plenitude and existential intensity.

❖

Silence halted and incarnated itself in Mary along with the Word. During these nine months, Mary did not need to pray, if by praying we mean to voice feelings or ideas. Never is communication so deep as when nothing is said, and never is silence so eloquent as when nothing is communicated.

Here, during these nine months, everything was still: "in" Mary and "with" Mary all is one: time, space, eternity, word, music, silence, Mary, God. Everything was assumed and divinized. *The Word was made flesh.*

A Few Scenes

On the night of the nativity, Mary was clothed in gentleness; silence was at its peak.

Here there is no house. No crib. No midwife. It is night. All is silence.

The night of the nativity was full of movement: the time had come to give birth; the Mother gave birth, wrapped the child in swaddling clothes and laid him in the manger. The music of the angels broke the silence of the night; the angel told the shepherds the news that the Awaited One had come, and gave them a sign to identify him. The shepherds said, "Let us go quickly." They arrived at the grotto, and found Mary and Joseph, and the Child lying in the manger. The shepherds must have offered them something to eat, or a gift of some kind; they spoke of all they had heard and seen during the night. Those who listened were astonished.

In the midst of all this, what did Mary do? "And Mary kept all these things, reflecting on them in her heart" (Lk 2:19). Ineffable sweetness, in the midst of an infinite happiness. And all in silence.

Many mothers, when they give birth, weep for joy. We can imagine the intensity of the happiness of Mary. Never is the experience so deep as when nothing is said.

❖

On a certain day there was a great commotion in the Temple of Jerusalem.

A venerable elderly man, touched by the Holy Spirit, took the Child in his arms. He said now he could die in peace because his eyes had contemplated the Awaited One, whose destiny was to destroy and to build, to overthrow and to lift up. He told the Mother that she should be prepared, for she too would be involved in the turmoil of this destiny of ruin and resurrection. Anna, a venerable octogenarian, felt suddenly rejuvenated, and began to say marvelous things about this Child.

What did Mary do in the midst of that general commotion? What did she say? "The child's father and mother were amazed at what was said about him" (Lk 2:33).

Mary must have lived these episodes so intensely that the names, the age and the words of these elders were engraved in her heart. After many years she transmitted it all, faithfully, to the early community.

❖

On Calvary, Mary was a touching figure of silence.

Calvary was full of funeral music, movement, voices, cosmic events: the cross, the nails, the soldiers, the robbers, the centurion, the Sanhedrin, an earthquake, the tearing of the Temple veil, the sudden darkness, mockeries, the last words of Jesus: "Forgive them, for they know not what they do.... This very night you will be with me in paradise.... Father, why have you abandoned me?... I am thirsty.... Here is your son, here is your mother.... Into your hands I commend my spirit; all is finished...."

In the midst of this pathetic symphony, what did Mary do? What did she say? "Standing by the cross of Jesus were his mother..." (Jn 19:25). In the center of this desolate scene, Mary stands, in silence and solitude, similar to a mute rock. No screams, no hysterics or fainting, possibly no tears.

The prophet Jeremiah had imagined her as a solitary cabin in the high mountain, beaten upon by violent winds.

Here on Calvary the silence of Mary is transformed into adoration. Never has silence meant so much as in this moment: surrender, availability, strength, fidelity, plenitude, elegance, fecundity, peace.... Never has a creature lived a moment with such existential intensity as Mary did on Calvary.

❖

In summary, we scarcely know anything of Mary. We do not know when she died, where she died, or even if she died. There are thousands of theories about the years that she lived, but all of them lack foundations.

There are a thousand theories about where she died. Some say in Ephesus, others in Smyrna, others in Jerusalem. None of these theories have any solid basis.

There are two theories about whether she died or if, without dying, she was lifted up into heaven in soul and body. Some say that Mary did not die because of her Immaculate Conception, since death is the penalty for sin. They hold that, without dying, she was assumed body and soul into heaven. Others say that she submitted to the law of death so as to imitate Jesus. She died and God raised her and lifted her soul and body into heaven.

Both groups hoped that Pius XII would give the final verdict on the occasion of the dogmatic definition of the Assumption in 1950. They supposed that the Pope, while proclaiming that Mary was lifted body and soul into heaven, would have to determine how this happened—that is, whether before dying or, once dead she was raised up. The moment came and Pius XII said nothing about this matter.

In history, Mary appears as if by surprise. She disappears at once, as someone of no importance. There is a famous, ancient song which says:

> And let us not forget
> that for a brief and brilliant moment,
> there was a Camelot.

For a brief and brilliant moment a Star appeared and said: "Only God is important." And the star disappeared.

PART FOUR
THE MOTHER

The name of this handsome young man
was written on the snow. At sunrise, the snow melted
and carried the name away on the waters.
—Kazantzakis

She gave birth to a Son for a sublime happiness.
And now she has lost herself in her silent sweetness.
—Hebbel

CHAPTER 10

The Mother of the Lord

The Eternal Mother

A legend of Brittany says that when boats are shipwrecked on the high seas and the sailors drown in deep waters, "Lady Death" whispers lullabies in their ears, the same songs they learned from their mothers when they were rocked in their cradles.

According to an oriental poem, the mother who has died returns every night to cradle her children, even if they are adults. All of nature—wind, trees, waves, shadows—is transformed into motherly arms which caress, welcome and defend these dear orphans.

A mother never dies. Gertrud Von Le Fort, a German author, says:

> In popular poetry on the mother, a deep kinship arises between birth and death.

Mother, grief, death, fecundity...these words are not only approximate or evocative. They are notions so intimately related, so mutually interdependent that in a certain sense they are synonymous.

A mother is everything at the same time: sacred and secular, rock and star, sunrise and sunset, mystery and flesh, sound and silence, strength and tenderness. She is like fertile soil, always giving birth and always burying the dead, tirelessly perpetuating life through immortal generations.

❖

To fulfill her destiny, sacred and human at the same time, the mother—to be a mother and on becoming a mother—renounces and loses her personality and is submerged in anonymity in the current of generations. The mother does not have a personal identity; she is simply, "the wife of William," "the mother of Johnny." Essentially, she is gift. She belongs to someone. She does not possess; she is possessed.

But as the hour of birth unfolds behind the curtain, so too does all heroism in the life of the mother. It glides on in deep simplicity, exempt of pathos. She suffers in silence. She weeps in secret. By night, she keeps watch. By day, she works. She is the candle; her children are the light. She gives birth like the soil, silently. Here is the root of her greatness and beauty.

Gibran says:

> We die so that we may give life, just as our fingers weave a cloth we will never wear.
>
> We throw the net to catch fish we will never taste.
> Our joy is placed in that which saddens us.

The mystery of Mary casts itself like a light upon the eternal mother who never dies and always survives. The figure of Mary as Mother assumes and summarizes the grief, the struggle and the hope of innumerable mothers who have perpetuated life on earth.

Between the Closing and the Opening

The Incarnation is simultaneously a closing and an opening.

On the one hand, it is the climax and culmination of overwhelming interventions of God effected over the centuries, particularly in favor of his people, Israel.

The God of the Bible, our God, is not an intellectual abstraction like law, order, power, will.... Our God is *Someone*. He is One who intervenes, enters the scene, compels events, erupts in the private precinct of the person but always to liberate. In a word, he is a *person*: he speaks, challenges, pleads, forgives, agrees, compromises, proposes, at times disposes. Above all, he is a God who loves, worries, cares: he is a *Father*.

On the other hand, the Incarnation is an *opening* to a kingdom that will never know sunset. Earthly kingdoms are born, grow and die within the inevitable biological cycle. The Church is the new theater of operations, the new Israel, belonging to God. Thus, as God is the eternal living One, without end, since he is above the biological process, so the Church, which is but a prolongation of the Incarnation, will last until the curtain falls and time ends.

The Incarnation opens a path which always leads onward and upward until it reaches the final culmination.

At this intersection of the closing and the opening, Mary stands with her *yes*.

Born of a Woman (Gal 4:4)

Matthew and Luke open their respective Gospels with lists of names, distasteful because of their dryness, called *genealogies*. Luke traces his on an ascending line, Matthew on a descending one.

Despite the fact that such genealogies are monotonous and usually left aside in the reading of the Bible, they contain a great concentration of meaning. They indicate that our God is not a primitive force or the cosmic order; he is a real God, although nameless—the God of Abraham, the God of Isaac, the God of Jacob. He is the Father of our Lord Jesus Christ.

> He is the One who from the old brings forth what is new, and what has been hoped for he fully realizes; he does not stop history but leads it to its fullness; he cooperates with human beings, and from their imperfect achievements, even from their failures, he produces a finished product.[1]

In Matthew's descending list, Mary is located at the end of the genealogy. Among the Jews, every genealogical tree advances rigorously along the masculine line, but here, at the end, is the name of a woman, Mary. How strange!

Mary appears here, however, as a necessary reference to Christ. Since the end and culmination of the list is Jesus Christ, and since Christ could not be conceived without Mary, then of necessity Matthew included Mary. In this way, Mary's entrance in the New Testament occurs at the end of a genealogy—because of a necessary reference to Someone. How like a Mother!

> ...Jacob the father of Joseph, the husband of Mary.
> Of her was born Jesus who is called the Messiah.
>
> *—Matthew 1:16*

Thus Mary, according to the Bible, is at the crossroads; she occupies a central place between humanity and God. The Son of God receives human nature from Mary and enters on the human scene through this channel.

The generations advance one after another until, invariably, they end in Christ, just as rivers flow into the sea. The whole movement of history converges and culminates in Christ: the Law, the prophets, the entire Word.

This being so, Christ appears in reference to Mary: "of her was born Jesus" (Mt 1:16). The Mother is named immediately before the Son. Mary is then the representative of the generations that preceded her and, at the same time, the door for future generations of the redeemed.

In a word, because she is Mother, Mary is, together with Christ, the center and the convergence of the history of salvation.

> We should mention the Mother of Christ as the place where the decisive passage of the eternal Son of God to human nature and human history was accomplished.
>
> The Mother is found between God and humanity. Here was realized the historical decision of salvation.[2]

Mother of God

The invariable doctrine of the Church teaches that Jesus Christ in his human nature was truly engendered by a human mother. Jesus Christ is in fact the Son of Mary. Just as any other mother supplies everything for the fruit of her womb, so did Mary supply the human nature with which the Word identified himself, and the fruit was Jesus Christ.

Within the scope and meaning of the dogma that was elaborated by the Church based on biblical data and defined by the Council of Ephesus, we affirm that Mary was not only the Mother of Christ *as man* but also Mother of Jesus Christ, the divine Person of the Word. This is the meaning of the first marian dogma proclaimed with great joy in Ephesus in the year 431. The Word is *her Son*, and Mary is *his Mother*, in the same way that other mothers are mothers of a complete person.

Hypothetically, the Word could have been incarnated by identifying himself consubstantially at a determined moment with an adult person. But, in fact, it did not happen this way. According to revealed truth, God entered into humanity through the normal channel of the biological process, beginning with the very first phases of a human embryo.

This is why we speak of the divine maternity. This is also why Elizabeth, overwhelmed, asked herself: "What is this? The Mother of my Lord—here?" St. Paul, speaking of the eternal Jesus Christ, says that he was "fashioned" in the womb of a woman (cf. Gal 4:4), and he uses an emphatic expression: born "according to the flesh" (Rom 1:3). The angel at the annunciation, in speaking to Mary about the identity of the One who will flourish in her womb, asserts that he is "Son of the Most High."

❖

Every person owes his or her existence to the engendering activity of a mother. An apple, for example, is a "fruit," a living being formed by the maternal principle which is an apple tree. The apple tree gave life to its "fruit" for a long time, until the fruit was ripe and could break away from the mother tree. But the human person is much more with respect to the mother than the fruit with respect to the tree. The fruit is not a subsistent being as is the human person. The apple, detached from the apple tree, is not autonomous and subsistent.

According to the doctrine of the Church, as "fruit," we are totally indebted to the maternal activity, but as *person*, we are not entirely the product of the engendering process, because our immortal soul comes directly from God Immortal. The maternal activity prepares a somatic constitution, a body, while God directly infuses his immortal breath, and this happens at the very first moment of conception.

But in the final analysis, the mother does not give life to a "fruit," but to a *person*. She is the mother of a person, body and soul. This explanation will facilitate our exposition of the divine maternity.

❖

In Mary's case, what occurred was a "personifying" process. "In" Mary, humanity and divinity became one, consubstantially. The human being, alone, is not the person of Christ; neither is the person of the Eternal Word the person of Jesus Christ. Only when both realities became one through the "hypostatic union," do we have the *Person of Jesus Christ*. There existed then a "personifying" process. And this process was carried out in the womb of Mary.

We could say that, simultaneously, humanity assumed divinity and divinity assumed humanity. This point of convergence, the central knot in the history of the world, was accomplished "in" Mary. With this perspective we can affirm without any hesitation that Mary is the center of history.

Speaking more precisely, we can say that Jesus Christ is "the God who became man." That would be the most exact translation of the name "Emmanuel." This is why we say so often that God manifested himself in Jesus Christ.

❖

As Scheeben,[3] a German theologian of the last century, wrote so clearly, the motherhood of Mary properly gives life to a man who is truly and really God. Therefore it would not be exact to say that Mary is the mother of a man who, *at the same time,* is God, as if her maternal activity touches directly and immediately, almost exclusively, the human in Christ. So as to avoid any confusion, it is imperative to assert that the direct and formal product of the engendering activity of Mary was the Man-God. This is what we mean when we say that Mary is the Mother of God.

From these premises we come to the conclusion that it would not be exact to think that Mary's generative collaboration was ordered primarily to the formation of the human nature of Christ as a mere man, and secondarily to the God-Man. This God-Man being a divine person, we conclude evidently that Mary's maternal activity had one finality, the divine existence of a man and at the same time the human existence of the Word.

According to Scheeben's reasoning, the Eternal Word comes to be the object of Mary's maternal activity, insofar as from her and in her, he clothes himself in flesh. Even more: the Word is so explicitly and directly the goal of Mary's maternal activity that we may affirm that this engendering process has no other finality than to "revest" the Word with the human flesh of Mary. Hence the strong expression of Paul, born "according to the flesh" (Rom 1:3).

The Word is, first of all, a divine Person who comes to possess a human nature, and secondly, a man in possession of divinity. All this is meant when we say that Mary is the Mother of God, *Theotokos*.

Birth is a symbol of motherhood, but in fact, it is only the *manifestation*—"the coming to light"—of a generative process brought about in the darkness of a mother's womb over nine months.

Born of the Virgin Mary

For centuries the Church has repeated words full of grandeur and majesty: *"Et incarnatus est de Spiritu Sancto ex Maria Virgine."* The mystery of the Incarnation! He (the Word) was made *flesh* "in" and "of" the Virgin Mary, by the work of the Holy Spirit.

This *flesh* which the Word assumed was "fabricated" through the creative and direct power of the Holy Spirit, and not within the normal biological process. Dogma and Scripture affirm further that this creative action of the Holy Spirit was realized concretely "in" and "of" Mary. The Latin preposition *"ex"* has a deeper sense and says much more than our prepositions "of" or "from."

The exceptional action of the Holy Spirit did not prescind the engendering activity of the Mother, but specifically required it—in such a way that there was a mutual cooperation between the Holy Spirit and the motherly activity of Mary: the one in the other, and the one at the side of the other. As Scheeben says, with great precision, Mary was a true principle of Christ's humanity, though subordinated to the Holy Spirit and operating under his action, and both—the Holy Spirit and Mary—worked in communion of action.

This activity on the part of Mary implied a biological collaboration and also a spiritual one which we will treat later.

Biologically, every mother, before sexual relations with her husband, prepares, or better, forms within herself an organic egg cell capable of being fertilized by the action of the man. And after, in a symbiotic process, the mother contributes food, oxygen—blood—through the umbilical cord until the fetus comes to maturity, detaches itself and is brought to light. This engendering collaboration of the mother is called gestation or pregnancy. Biologically, birth has no importance, it is simply a release.

❖

In this maternal process, dogma, following Scripture, on the one hand excludes natural fertilization, and, on the other, affirms the engendering activity of Mary.

In the human process, the father cooperates in the formation of the corporal substance by means of the sperm. In contrast, in the generation of Jesus Christ, the cooperative action flowed from the exceptional operation of the creative power of God over the human substance uniquely provided by Mary.

This action, according to Scripture, consisted in an "invasion" by the Holy Spirit, and in an "action" of the infinite power of God (cf. Lk 1:35). Scripture uses some very beautiful expressions to convey the meaning of this action: it says that the *shadow* of the Most High will *cover* Mary. They are noble expressions which bring to mind certain natural elements whose action leaves intact the subject over which it acts, such as light, mist, shadow, dew.

In a word, in the engendering process of the Incarnation, the Holy Spirit is, mysteriously, the *agent* who provides the creative power which flows from the fount of the Most High.

The Meaning of the Virgin Birth

If Scripture and Tradition affirm with such insistence the fact of the virginal maternity, what would God's reasons be for such a strange and exceptional option in the history of humanity?

In the first place God, with this fact, wishes to establish most clearly and strikingly that the only Father of our Lord Jesus Christ is God himself. Jesus Christ was not born by the will of blood, nor by any carnal desire, but by the will of God.

Moreover, with the fact of the virgin birth, the biological process which comes from Adam—and from the most distant frontiers of biogenesis—is broken and transcended. An old order is interrupted for the first and only time, in order to show that, with the arrival of Jesus Christ, a new plan is established—not one of generation through sex, but that of regeneration through resurrection.

The virginity of Mary is the symbol, figure and model of the virginity of the Church, especially of that definitive and heavenly Church. This heavenly Church is nothing other than an innumerable multitude of virgins, where love has reached its fullness, sex has become entirely sublime, and the victorious will not marry nor be given in marriage. A new homeland, a new order, a new love. Christ transforms everything. The Transformer had to come into the world in a different and virginal way; he had to live and die in a different and virginal manner. "I am the one who makes everything new," says the book of Revelation.

The Virgin Mary is an image of the virgin Church. The roads over which liberators travel in the middle of the night are roads of solitude. Every woman desires to have children, someone nearby who can give her protection, affection and security. She wants clothes to show off, jewels to display, a house to make her home. The virgin is a solitary traveler who ventures forth on a cold night. She is a solitary but fascinating figure. Her solitude contains a hidden splendor: she is God's territory, an exclusive heritage of the Lord; he alone has access to and dominion over her. This was the Virgin Mary, and such must be the virgin Church: pathways of faith, humility, poverty, service, availability—along with persecutions, struggles and hopes.

Virginity means all of this.

❖

According to the angel of the annunciation, the One who was to germinate in Mary's womb would be "holy" (Lk 1:35), and the Holy One to be born from her would sanctify her.

In the Bible, "holy" is not an adjective, a quality or a property; it is a noun. The word "holy," as Schelkle translates so well, means: "drawn away from the world with God and by God." In its semantic sense, "holy" refers to verbs such as to separate, reserve, set apart.

It is there that we can ponder the profound significance of virginity: someone allured by God, inserted solitarily in the heart of night, remaining upright, sustained only by the strong arm of the Father and illumined by the veiled radiance of his face.

> Originally, God is holy, inasmuch as he is separated from the world; he is totally distinct from it.
>
> One is holy who, separated from this world, belongs to the world of God.
>
> Thus Mary, through the holiness of her Son, is herself holy. She is withdrawn from the limit of the created, and located in the sphere of the things and persons that God has made his.
>
> This is why Joseph has no sexual relations with Mary.[4]

The virgin birth is something so unheard of that it can only be accepted if we see it as one of the great salvific gestures. "It is something inconceivable that a human being receive life without the engendering act of a father; accepting this fact superficially would be a sign of mere indifference and not necessarily faith," says Schelkle.[5]

The virgin birth is one of the greatest marvels in the history of salvation, if not the greatest, and within that melody there rings throughout the Bible: "Nothing is impossible for God" (cf. Gn 18:14; Lk 1:37).

> The miracle of the birth of Christ without a father is precisely the revelation of the freedom and creative action of God.

> Even in Christ's corporeality is found this announcement: now begins something new, which is absolutely a creative action of God and proof of his power.

> In this sense we can interpret that assertion of Paul (cf. 1 Cor 15:45-47) that Christ, as a new Adam, as the chief and the head of a new humanity, was not formed from the earth but proceeds from heaven and is a giver of life.

> Christ, the human creature, has no father. Jesus Christ-Man is a direct work of God. Only to him belongs the glory of the work and life of Jesus.[6]

❖

All of us live enshrouded in an atmosphere of Freudian inspiration, in a more and more secularized society. The myth of sex has been exalted so much that even believers begin to feel a certain uneasiness as regards the virgin birth. They have no difficulty in accepting facts much more sensational such as the Resurrection, but they feel some sort of annoyance before this other fact of salvation. They forget that we are confronting a matter of faith.

The judgment on the tradition of the virgin birth and its acceptance is definitely part of the tradition of Jesus Christ, and part of the affirmation of this tradition.

If, then, Christ is the only beloved Son and the true image of God; if he is the consummation of the new era, as the necessary act for lost humanity, the total renewal and the strength, the way, the truth and the life...then, the affirmation of the nonexistence of an earthly father encompasses a profound mystery.

The New Testament texts which refer to the virginal maternity trace a limited lineage which is barely perceptible concerning the reality of Jesus Christ, limited yet well determined, and despite the scantiness of the texts, it is worthy of acceptance; it leaves an impression on and becomes unforgettable to the reader.[7]

Mary, During the Months of Her Pregnancy

To know Mary's feelings during the days of her pregnancy, let us place ourselves before similar situations.

If today we ask a pregnant woman who is at the same time a woman of deep faith with a true interior life, what feelings she experiences in her pregnancy, she will not know what to respond. What she is going through is not strange, it is unfathomable! Finally, with difficulty, she will speak. Even if her words are hesitant, however, she will be able to evoke an ineffable world, a world that is born and which dies with her maternity.

What was Mary's psychic and spiritual stature during those days of pregnancy? In the scene of the annunciation, Mary appears to be endowed with an exceptional maturity and capacity for reflection, and above all, a deep spirituality—and all this in proportions that do not correspond to her age.

If we measure her spiritual stature by the content of the "Magnificat," we confirm that when the personal mystery of the Lord God is evoked, Mary becomes a vibrant young woman and even exalted, despite the fact that ordinarily she is reserved and silent. She knows the history of Israel, and she is fully conscious of the meaning of the Incarnation. Besides, she is Immaculate, full of grace, inhabited by the substantial presence of the Word, and under the direct influence of the Holy Spirit.

Such is the one who is to live a unique experience.

❖

With difficulty will the mind conceive, the tongue express and the most penetrating intuition guess the breadth and depth of Mary's intimacy with God during this time. During these nine months, Mary's interior world must have been powerfully enriched on the physical, psychic and spiritual levels.

It must have been unique and ineffable.

Mary lives immersed in a limitless universe, always looking contemplatively toward the center of her being where the infinite mystery of the Incarnation is realized. Her entire body and whole soul were centered and concentrated on her magnificent Lord who was dwelling within her.

Physiology admirably describes how all the vital functions of a pregnant woman converge on the little creature at the center of her organism, and cooperate in its formation. While in Mary the physiological functions were spontaneously directed to the center of her organism where the Son of God grew, Mary's whole soul—its awareness, emotions, vital energies—also converged freely and devotedly on this same center, the theater of the marvels of God.

❖

In any maternity clinic the following phenomenon can be proven with a spectroscope: when the mother is emotionally moved, the child in her womb is moved also. If the mother's heartbeat is accelerated, so also is the child's. If the heart of the mother is at rest, so is the heart of the baby. All of the successive emotions of the mother are lived by the small creature and can be detected by the spectroscope.

Accordingly, in this case the Creator and the creature lived off the same blood; the Lord and the servant were fed with the same food and breathed the same oxygen. Thus, as their bodies were only one body according to the phenomenon of symbiosis, in the same way their spirits were only one: the attention of Mary and the "attention" of God were mutually interlocked, producing an indescribable intimacy. Mary was entirely lost in the total presence of the Lord God.

All of Mary's mental energies remained concentrated on the One who was "with her," on the One who was the soul of her soul and life of her life. During these moments, Mary's prayer did not consist in expressing words; nor was it, strictly speaking, a reflection, because in a reflection there exists a mental movement, a process of distinguishing and of connecting.

In Mary, during these moments of deep intimacy with her Lord, there is no movement of the mind; all is quiet. What is it? An act? A state? An instant? A situation? Whatever the case, *all* of Mary (all of her mental energies integrated) in one simple and total act (attitude?), "remains" *in* God, *with* God, *inside* God and God *inside her*.

This might be the appropriate expression: *all* of Mary remains mute *in her* Son-God.

It was a deep and penetrating intimacy. During these moments of intense contemplation Mary had no images, no set thoughts. Such thoughts make an absent person present in the mind, but in the case of Mary's pregnancy, there was no need to make an absent one present, because he was there "with" her. He was Presence, identified with her body and soul.

In spite of this identification, Mary preserved the consciousness of her own identity, and more and better than ever she measured the distance between the majesty of her Lord and the littleness of his grateful servant.

❖

The Holy Spirit brought the creative force of the Almighty to form a substantial body in Mary's womb. The action of the Holy Spirit was not limited to the initial forming of the embryo, leaving it to continue its transformation into a human organism on its own. He did not retire as one who has accomplished his mission. Rather, he accompanied it with his influence throughout the process of pregnancy.

Now, here we encounter a mystery before which the human imagination is confounded. Mary received the Person of the Eternal Word, the second Person of the Trinity. At the same time, she received the Holy Spirit, not only in his effects, as on the day of Pentecost, but as a Person.

Thus Mary was, strictly speaking, the temple of the Blessed Trinity. It is true that God is not restricted to space or time, yet the intratrinitarian communications were active within Mary, within the confines of her bodily dimensions. How was this done? Here, we are at a loss.

"In" Mary, during these nine months, the Father was *Fatherhood*, that is, he continued his eternal process of begetting his Son. The Son, who was *Sonship*, continued in turn the eternal process of "being begotten." And from the embrace of both, the Holy Spirit was proceeding. From eternity to eternity the same marvel was happening: in the closed circle of the intratrinitarian realm a vital, fertile current of knowledge and love was flowing, an ineffable life of abundant sharing between the three Persons. This tremendous mystery was now unfolding within the limited frame of this fragile young woman. It is far beyond imagination.

The total and Trinitarian mystery was embracing, penetrating, possessing and occupying the whole of Mary. Was the young mother conscious of all that was happening within her? It is always the same: the greater the depth of an experience, the less the capacity to conceptualize it and still less the capacity to express it. According to the spirituality of the *poor of Yahweh*, Mary had unconditionally surrendered herself to God, and now there was only one possible attitude: to be continually receptive. Her concern was not to understand, but to be faithful.

❖

Nevertheless, Mary was not an alienated pregnant mother. Pseudo-contemplation alienates. But true contemplation gives maturity, common sense and productivity. It is true that Mary was submerged in the presence of God. But in this presence she kept her feet firmly on the ground. She knew that she had to eat more because the One to be born was sharing her food.

Further, for Mary, to live lost in the Lord meant to live in the midst of the total human and earthly reality.

She begins to prepare, to weave (not buy) the swaddling clothes for the One who was to come. She looks after the complicated preparations for the "nuptial procession," the marriage ceremony. On the determined day she goes through that ritual which takes her to Joseph's house. So as to avoid the popular curse that would particularly hurt her Son, she conceals the visible effects of her pregnancy and, very possibly for the same reason, hastened her trip to Bethlehem.

The presence of God awakens above all fraternal sensitivity. The young woman goes to Elizabeth's house to congratulate her, to help her through the last months of pregnancy and in the tasks of childbirth. God is like that. He never leaves one in peace. He uproots. He always draws the person from her own circle to launch her into service and kindness toward the needy of this world.

❖

Never before has a mother of such sweetness, tenderness and silence been seen. Never again on this earth will we see the figure of a woman so evocatively ineffable, with such a deep spirituality. All the women of the world, past and future, will discover their highest expression in this young mother.

All mothers who have died in childbirth are revived here, in the womb of this pregnant Mother, to give birth along with her to future generations.

The voices and melodies of the universe composed here, in this young Mother, a complete and immortal symphony.

The pregnant woman who appears in the glorious vision of the Apocalypse, standing over the moon, clothed with the sun and crowned with stars, is Mary (cf. Rev 12:1-15).

The Son, a Portrait of His Mother

We know little about Mary. The New Testament is sparing in words referring to her. Despite the fact that we sense her presence in the Gospels, her figure is lost in the shadows, and we have to wander through deductions and intuitions if we are to capture the person and personality of Mary.

In spite of this precariousness, we nevertheless have a sure source of information: her own Son. All of us are a product of the combined inclinations and tendencies of our father and mother, transmitted through the "Mendelian laws."

Physiognomic as well as psychic characteristics are transmitted from parents to children through genetic codes. In the interior of the cell of the ovum are "threads" called *chromosomes*. Each chromosome in turn is formed of small elements linked like a chain. These elementary corpuscles, called *genes*, are the carriers of the parental traits. Forming different formulas or genetic combinations, these genes are what determine a great part of the physiognomy and psychological tendencies transmitted by the parents and inherited by the children. The secret mystery by which the paternal and maternal chromosomes form a genetic code is not yet known, but we do know that it is through these codes that the characteristics of the parents are transmitted.

Now, Christ had no father in the genetic sense of the word. Hence, in his case, the transmission and reception of the physiognomy and psychological traits came through only one channel, from only one source—his Mother.

Consequently, there must have been a great physical resemblance between the Mother and Son. The reactions and general behavior of Mary and Jesus must have been very similar. This comes out clearly in the Gospels. What was Mary like? We have only to look at Jesus. The Son was the "double" of his Mother—her photograph, her exact image, in physical appearance as well as in psychic reactions.

❖

There are other very interesting aspects in the Gospels which enable us to know, deductively, who the Mother was and what she was like. In the first place, Jesus is the One Sent, the One who, before proclaiming the beatitudes, lived them himself to their ultimate consequences.

In the second place, Jesus was this Son who, from the time of his infancy, observed and admired in his Mother that complete set of human attitudes—humility, patience, fortitude—that he was later to proclaim as beatitudes on the mountain. I say this because every time Mary appears in the Gospels she presents those characteristics described in the sermon on the Mount: patience, humility, fortitude, peace, meekness, mercy....

All of us are to some degree what our mother was. A true mother recreates and forms her child in a certain sense to her own image and profile, in terms of ideals, convictions and lifestyle. It must have made a deep impression on Jesus to have observed, admired and imitated, from his earliest years, that silence, that dignity and peace, that secret of not being upset by adversities, which he saw in his mother.

For me it is evident that at the sermon on the Mount, Jesus, consciously or unconsciously, aware or unaware, did nothing other than portray the spiritual figure of his Mother which rose from the depths of his subconscious, prompted by memories which reached back to his first years. The beatitudes are a photograph of Mary.

❖

In the pages of the Gospels we glimpse as through shadows an impressive parallelism between the spirituality of Jesus and that of his Mother.

In the decisive moment of her life, Mary fixed her destiny with the words, *"May it be done"* (Lk 1:38). When his "hour" came, Jesus fixed the destiny of his life and the salvation of the world with words of the same meaning, "...not what I will but what you will" (Mk 14:36). That expression symbolizes and summarizes a vast spirituality which embraces the entire life with its impulses and commitment in line with the *poor of Yahweh*.

When Mary wishes to express her spiritual identity, her "personality" before God and humanity, she does it with these words: "I am the handmaid of the Lord" (Lk 1:38). When Jesus proposes himself as a model to be imitated, he uses the words "meek and humble" (Mt 11:29). According to scholars, these two expressions have the same meaning, they have the same content, once more, within the spirituality of the *poor of Yahweh.*

Mary affirms that the Lord dethroned the powerful and elevated the humble (cf. Lk 1:52). Jesus says that the proud will be humbled and the humble exalted.

From these and other parallels we encounter in the Gospels, we may conclude that Mary had an extraordinary and definitive influence on the life and spirituality of Jesus; that much of the gospel inspiration is due to Mary as to a distant fountain; that the Mother was an excellent teacher, her pedagogy consisting not so much in many words but in living intensely a determined spirituality with which she imbued her Son since childhood, and that, finally, the Gospel is in general a distant echo of the life of Mary.

A Hastened Trip

Tradition and popular imagination have supposed for centuries that Mary made her trip from Nazareth to Bethlehem a few days before the birth. The immense majority of authors, including the present one, have accepted this supposition without giving it much thought. Paul Gechter has a very different opinion, based on the gospel context. His conclusion confers on Mary a singular greatness.[8]

According to the medical evangelist, St. Luke, Mary and Joseph, now married, felt obliged to make this trip to Bethlehem under the pressure of an imperial edict (cf. Lk 2:1). This reason does not exclude that the trip may have had other motives.

The succession of events might have been something like this: three months after the annunciation, Mary returns from Ain Karim to Nazareth. One day, we do not know when, Joseph receives the explanation of what happened to Mary. From Matthew 1:24, we have the impression that the "nuptial procession," was held as soon as possible, immediately after Joseph was notified. The procession could have taken place between the fourth and fifth month after the annunciation, that is, a short time before the first visible symptoms of pregnancy.

Behind this haste we suspect Joseph's preoccupation and fear that very soon the popular curse against Mary was about to ignite.

If Joseph wanted to defend Mary's good name, and especially the Son's name, he had to leave Nazareth quickly. The occasion of the imperial census, which must have been promulgated many months before, presented him with a God-sent solution. The imperial order was providential for them because with it their departure from Nazareth at this time would not seem strange to anyone (cf. Mt 2:22).

Thus we can better appreciate the veiled intention behind Luke's expression that Mary was "with child" (Lk 2:5). This indication implies that the pregnancy was the reason for hastening the trip. Mary had to depart from Nazareth as soon as possible. In Bethlehem, no one would pay any attention to the fact that Mary was pregnant because no one would have known the time of their marriage. Gechter goes on to say: "Thus, over the Incarnation of Jesus a veil was extended that hid the mystery from the Nazareans and from the Bethlehemites."

Luke does not say: "When they arrived there the days for giving birth were accomplished," but "while they were there" (Lk 2:6). Luke's text, therefore, leaves a wide margin for determining the chronology of Jesus' birth. If the delivery took place immediately after their arrival or some time later, the text does not say.

According to this reasoning, Mary and Joseph could have traveled from Nazareth to Bethlehem around the fifth month after the annunciation.

Be that as it may, in either of these two suppositions, the situation of Mary was not idyllic. In either case, she had to live in a humanly difficult situation. But here lies Mary's greatness. When a person lives immersed in God and abandoned to his will, as she lived, that person experiences a deep peace and security even in the midst of a furious tempest. Any one of us can confirm this; when one lives the presence of God intensely, then one fears nothing and feels tremendously free, and, come what may, one lives in an unbreakable peace.

The threatening situations that surrounded Mary did not obstruct in any degree the depth, meekness and intimacy which Mary experienced throughout these months. It is a lesson on life.

CHAPTER 11

A Divine Pedagogy

There has always been a shocking phenomenon for me vaguely visible between the lines of the Gospels: the way Jesus treated his mother. His relationship with her is not similar to that of other sons with their mothers. Whenever Mary appears in the Gospels with him, Jesus deliberately takes a cold and distant attitude in her regard. A very deep mystery is hidden behind this attitude, one we will try to unveil through this chapter. It was a mysterious pedagogy.

It is useless to alter the meaning of the words by trying to soften the harshness of some of the gospel expressions. Jesus is not an ungrateful son. Why did he behave that way? Mary appears in the Gospels as the supreme expression of delicacy and kindness; she did not deserve such treatment. Why did all of this happen?

A compact theology pulsates here which adorns the gospel message with unsuspected depth. In this context, Mary's behavior attains such grandeur that one remains simply overcome with amazement before this incomparable woman.

"The flesh is of no avail" (Jn 6:63)

Jesus Christ had come to transform everything. He had come to draw us from the world of the flesh to place us in the realm of the Spirit. With his coming, all blood relations would be annulled and frontiers of the spirit would be established within which God would be Father of us all and we would all become brothers and sisters to one another (cf. Mt 23:8).

Further, for all those who radically embrace the will of the Father, God becomes father, mother, spouse, brother, sister... (cf. Mt 12:50; Lk 8:21). All that is human is not suppressed; it is sublimated. This was the revolution of the Spirit.

All human reality moves in closed circles. Jesus Christ came to open humankind to unlimited horizons. For example, fatherhood, motherhood, the home and human love revolve in closed circles. Jesus Christ wished to open these realities to perfect love, to a paternal, maternal, fraternal universality.... In a word, he came to introduce the sphere of the Spirit.

❖

Jesus himself is consistent with his principles. At the hour set by his Father he leaves the familiar sphere of Nazareth. His permanent inclination is to withdraw from family, clan, province. He goes out to work first in Galilee, then in Samaria and later in Judea, each time further from the family nucleus. Apparently he did not want to return to his village.

Intuition and experience had brought him to this conclusion: wherever the prophet had established blood relations or neighborhood friendships, he was always looked upon with *"carnal eyes"*; there would be curiosity toward him but not faith. All of the fruit of the sowing would be wasted because the prophet has no prestige in his own land, among his own folks and in his own house (cf. Mk 6:5; Mt 13:57). In reality, "the flesh is of no avail" (Jn 6:63).

According to the Gospels, Jesus had experienced a sour disappointment in his own town and among his own relatives. The words of the Gospels are surprising: "He was amazed at their lack of faith" (Mk 6:6). "And he did not work many miracles there" (cf. Mt 13:58).

❖

The gospel texts progress invariably in the same direction, lifting people from the narrow margins of their small world to the loftiest heights: "If you greet only your brothers, how do you differ from the pagans?" (cf. Mt 5:47) "...Anyone who, in my name, leaves home, parents, brothers or sisters, will know what it means to be free and to be happy" (cf. Mt 19:29). "...Who are my disciples? If you are not capable of sacrificing your dearest realities for me—spouse, brothers, sisters, children—you cannot belong to my company of disciples." "...Do you believe that I have come to bring peace? I came to bring a sword, and to separate son from father, daughter from mother" (cf. Mt 10:35).

It is necessary to be born. What is born of the flesh is flesh; in its biological cycle it will end and decay. What is born of the Spirit is immortal like God himself (cf. Jn 3:1-10).

This is where we find the profound explanation for Jesus' coldness toward his mother, an attitude which, on the other hand, has a strictly pedagogical character.

A New Birth

After his resurrection, Jesus Christ will establish the kingdom of the Spirit: the Church. She is not primarily a human institution but a community of people who were born, not through the desire of the flesh nor of blood, but from God himself (cf. Jn 1:13). She is the people of the children of God born of the Spirit.

On Pentecost there will be a new birth. Jesus will be born a second time, not according to the flesh as in Bethlehem, but according to the Spirit. There is no birth without a mother. If the birth were spiritual, the mother would have to be spiritual. Humanly speaking, the mother is a sweet reality. This sweet reality must die by means of a transforming evolution, because for each birth there is also a death.

Thus Mary would have to experience a "passage." In a certain sense, she would have to forget that she was a mother according to the flesh. Her behavior, or rather, the mutual relationship between Mother and Son, would have to develop as though they were strangers to one another.

In a word, Mary would also have to leave the maternal realm, enclosed in itself, the sphere of the flesh, so as to enter into the sphere of faith. All of this was necessary because Christ needed a Mother in the Spirit for his second birth on Pentecost. The Church is the living prolongation of Jesus Christ, launched and spread over the length of history.

Thus Jesus adopts a peculiar pedagogy and submits his Mother to a process of transformation, a process which is always painful.

In the pre-adolescent period he was still a child, needing attention and maternal care. Now Jesus Christ, the Son of God and Son of Mary, enters resolutely into the cold region of human solitude. He detaches himself from his Mother as a large branch breaks off a tree; he declares himself to be exclusively the Son of God. He disregards his Mother's preoccupation and attests, without saying so, that the flesh is of no avail. This was an unexpected blow which upset the Mother deeply and painfully. She remained silent, keeping these things in her heart (cf. Lk 2:46-51).

Here Mary's composure crumbles. Jesus declares, in effect, that God alone is important, that God alone is worth it all, that God alone is sweetness and tenderness. In a tense environment, he proclaims from then on and forever the indisputable supremacy and exclusivity of the Lord God, the Father, beyond all human and earthly realities. Jesus takes again the rugged and solitary path of the great prophets: God alone!

❖

After this, Jesus manifests repeatedly his resolution not to accept motherly cares and affections (cf. Mk 3:20-35). If Mary wishes to express her communion with Jesus of Nazareth, it will not be in her capacity as a human mother; rather she will have to enter into a new relationship of faith and the Spirit. What had been said about the "sword" might refer to these realities, might it not?

With different events which were so many psychological blows, Jesus was elevating Mary through painful and disconcerting, yet transforming paths until the day of Pentecost in the "upper room." In the house of Jerusalem (cf. Acts 1:13), the Mother is there presiding over the group of those committed. They are waiting in hope for the Holy Spirit, who, *with* Mary and *in* Mary, will give birth to Jesus Christ for the second time and, this time, in the Spirit. The holy Church of God was born, through the work of the Holy Spirit, of the Virgin Mary.

For this moment Mary had already completed her paschal itinerary, she had realized the new spiritual childbirth, and now, again, she was *the Mother.* Mother in the faith and in the Spirit, the universal Mother of the Church, Mother of humanity and of history.

Not a Conflict, But a Pedagogy

Relations between Jesus and Mary did not unfold according to the usual pattern of a mother and child. In the present case, it is the Child and not the Mother who takes the initiative and decides what sort of mutual relations they are to have. This was true from the beginning. In his narrative of the infancy, Matthew emphasizes, on five different occasions, the meaningful expression "the Child and his Mother." This is not normal. However, the Gospels' objective is not to transmit what is normal in the relationship of a mother with her child but rather to transmit what was extraordinary and even strange.

In Mary's case, motherhood was not a joyful reality, exempt from conflicts. Mary was the *sorrowful Mother*— from the day of the annunciation, not only at the foot of the cross.

The distance that we feel exists between Jesus and Mary was not a psychological distance, but one of a different and very mysterious sort. Mary did not understand some expressions of and about Jesus; she felt uneasy with others. That "sword" must have been hanging over her soul like a threatening enigma. She had to flee to a foreign land. She lost the Child; rather the Child estranged himself willfully; he ran away from her protection. One day, as an adult, he deliberately left. Another day, the Son disappeared, devoured by the flames of disaster on Calvary.

A whole chain of events mark the paschal passage of the Mother *in a crescendo,* like a purifying process, toward a universal and spiritual maternity.

In this singular pedagogical process we meet another particularly intense event at Cana of Galilee. A wedding was the pinnacle feast in the family life of the Jews. In the present case, Jesus attended with his disciples. Mary was also there. Possibly they were among relatives.

Mary was attentive to every detail so that the feast would conclude to the satisfaction of all concerned. The celebration went on for a few days. At a certain moment Mary noticed that the wine was running out. She wanted to solve the negligence on her own, delicately and unnoticeably. She took the most direct shortcut and, approaching Jesus, told him what was happening. Her communication hid a humble plea: "Please, solve this predicament."

Jesus' answer was strange and distant. It sounded as though a ship were being broken in half. Mary had approached him with the assurance that she was in a human communion with him and that she would be granted a favor: it was a mother's request. Christ erected the wall of separation, beginning with the cold word: "woman." "The two of us have nothing in common; we are strangers to one another" (cf. Jn 2:4).

As much as we would like to soften the harshness of the answer, we cannot sidestep, according to the best scholars, the hardness of the words. However, had this episode been somewhat scandalous, the evangelist would not have reported it. Therefore there must be a great teaching hidden in the perplexity of this scene. In a careful analysis of the context, we must keep in mind that in the end Jesus did grant the favor to his Mother. The fact is that he advised his Mother not to be impatient, because his hour had not yet come. Thus, in its context, the episode seems to radiate more solemnity than coldness, as Lagrange suggests.

We can therefore conclude, agreeing with the best authors, that the literal sense of the words in John 2:4 is in accordance with our present reflection: "Dear Mother, the will of the 'flesh' cannot determine *my hour;* only the will of my Father can. We have entered into the era of faith and of the Spirit." Gechter writes:

> It is almost impossible to assert that "woman" takes the place of the word "mother." Rather it displaces it. Jesus has consciously rejected the natural relations which bound him to his mother by not taking them into account.
>
> Jesus wishes to say before anything else: "As my Mother on earth, you do not enter into the picture; you do not have any influence over me or my behavior."[9]

❖

The three synoptics underline another event as a new psychological blow. Mary went to search for Jesus, surely to take care of him, because the Lord did not even have time to eat (cf. Mk 3:20). This happened in Capernaum. Mark says Jesus was teaching in a house which was so full of people that Jesus' Mother and relatives were not able to get near him. Mary sent a message and they passed it on to Jesus: "Your mother and your brothers [and your sisters] are outside asking for you" (Mk 3:32).

Jesus, again transcending the human level, lifts his voice so that the Mother can hear it perfectly, and raises a question: "Who are my mother and [my] brothers?" And looking over all those who were surrounding him he said, "Here are my mother and my brothers. [For] whoever does the will of God is my brother and sister and mother" (Mk 3:33, 34-35; cf. Mt 12:46-50; Lk 8:19-21).

Was this a conflict? No! Disrespect toward his Mother? No! It was a new chapter in the purifying and transforming movement toward a universal motherhood. Mary understood Jesus, in an act of faith. Her whole life, as we have seen, was a fulfillment of the will of God with a unique perfection, always repeating her "May it be done." She was, then, doubly the Mother of Jesus.

On another occasion—was Mary present?—Jesus had just finished speaking when a woman in the midst of the crowd lifted her voice spontaneously: "How happy the woman who gave you birth and nourished you!" Jesus, again rising above human realities, replied: "Much happier are those who hear my word and put it into practice!" (cf. Lk 11:27) What does Luke say in another place? On two occasions (cf. Lk 2:19; 2:51) the evangelist underscores the fact that Mary kept and lived the Word. Therefore, Mary is doubly blessed—because she is the Mother and because she puts the Word into practice.

❖

Mary traveled this desolate *via dolorosa,* clothed in dignity and silence. She was simply magnificent. She was never demanding; she never protested. Elsewhere we have analyzed this behavior in full detail. When she did not understand certain words, she kept them in her heart and analyzed them serenely. To some rough scenes, she responded with sweetness and silence. Never did she break down. Throughout the journey she maintained the stature and elegance of an oak tree which remains the more firm and solid because it is beaten by stronger winds. She came to understand step by step that maternity in the Spirit is more important than that according to the flesh.

In this sense and because of this journey, we comprehend the deep relationship which exists between the virgin birth and fertile virginity. Those who are serious about complying with the will of the Father display all the elements of blood relationships, says Jesus: they are at the same time, mother, spouse, brother, sister....

Mary, while living in faith and in the Spirit and not according to the flesh, acquired the right of a universal motherhood over all the children of the Church who are born of the Spirit. Virginity is a maternity according to the Spirit, and it is in the sphere of the Spirit that virgins develop their fecundity. So, though the fecundity of human motherhood is enclosed within certain limits, virginal maternity opens her fecundity to a limitless universality. It is in this manner that Mary is both the model of the Church and a fertile virgin.

CHAPTER 12

Our Mother

Standing by the Cross

Again we need to have recourse to a brief yet complete story: "Standing by the cross of Jesus were his mother..." (Jn 19:25).

Mary's personality impresses us by its humility and courage. All through her life she managed to remain hidden in the shadows in a supporting role. When the hour of humiliation arrives, she advances and places herself in the forefront, dignified and silent. Mark tells us that on Calvary there were some "women looking on from a distance" (Mk 15:40). Meanwhile John specifies that the Mother remained standing by the cross.

The Romans, executors of the sentence and guardians of order, normally kept people at a prudent distance from the crucified criminals. But on some exceptional occasions they would permit very close relatives to approach those executed. This is why we find Mary near the cross at a solemn moment of her life and of the life of the Church.

❖

The scene in John 19:25-28 and the words, "Behold, your son," "Behold, your mother"—give us the impression, at first sight, that Jesus commits Mary to John's care. Jesus was departing and the Mother was without a spouse or sons who could shelter and care for her. She was left alone, and for the Jews, a woman left alone in life was a sign of chastisement. This is why Jesus, before dying, delicately took care of his Mother's future. This is the first impression.

But in the present scene there is an accumulation of circumstances which suggest that this scene of John with the Mother contains a much broader application and a much deeper significance than a mere family gesture.

Since the spiritual maternity of Mary is born here, we need to analyze in detail this complex of circumstances appointing her to a mission which is not simply of domestic but of messianic importance.

A Messianic Context

The episode we are going to analyze is placed in the midst of a series of narratives which all have a messianic sense, that is, they go beyond the simple narration of literal fact. John was a witness present at the cross. For his narrative he therefore made use of abundant material different from the synoptic narratives. In fact, John chose exclusively those facts which had a messianic significance, or at least tended to be messianic. Here are those facts.

❖

The Sanhedrin arrived at the Antonian fortress before the Roman governor. They manifested their annoyance at the ambiguity of the title on the cross and demanded that it be rectified. The governor finds their pretension ridiculous and categorically maintains his decision. Immediately after this we find ourselves again on

Calvary and we witness such minute details as the casting of dice for the robe, an event in which John sees the fulfillment of the Scriptures.

Again to fulfill the Scriptures, Jesus makes known his thirst. Jesus' thirst is not primarily of a physiological dimension. It is a completely natural phenomenon in one who has lost so much blood. However, the solution is not to give him water but a transfusion of blood. In this way, John continues selecting those scenes which do not end where the phenomenon finishes, rather they begin precisely where the phenomenon ends. The narcotic which the guard offers Jesus has a humanitarian purpose, to anesthetize the pain.

The last episode narrated is the breaking of the legs of the crucified and the piercing in Jesus' side by the centurion's lance, both of which happened to fulfill the Scriptures.

We are therefore seeing that John wants to offer a series of significant episodes without any internal logic. He does not pretend to offer us a narration, for, between ourselves, he is a poor narrator. When he writes, he is thinking about more than he describes. He wishes to demonstrate that the events which happened on the cross have fulfilled the Scriptures. Thus his aim is not really to inform by means of a coherent and well ordered narrative. It is in the center of five such passages that he places the episode of Mary and John.

Something More Than a Family Arrangement

According to a very general interpretation, we repeat, Jesus would have acted in the present scene like an only son who is preoccupied with the abandonment that will befall his mother. In his last moment he ensures the future of his solitary Mother.

We will underscore here the circumstances by which it appears clear that in Jesus' mind, there existed much deeper purposes and perspectives.

❖

In a careful analysis of the text it is important that we keep in mind that Jesus established a double current: one descending from Mary to John, "Behold, your son," and another ascending from John to Mary, "Behold, your mother." If it were only a family arrangement, we would be witness to a useless duplication, both from a grammatical and a psychological point of view.

If Jesus had only wanted to declare testamentary measures regarding the life of his Mother, it would have been sufficient to establish only one current, that of John with Mary: "John, take my Mother under your care until the end of her life." That would have been enough. He could have avoided the rest. Why establish a current from Mary to John? That would be superfluous.

To follow up with the analysis of the parallel expressions—"Behold, your son," "Behold, your mother"—if we remain on an ordinary human level, Jesus would have been acting with little consideration for his Mother. Why?

It was natural and in good form that Jesus should earnestly solicit John in his last hour: "John, take good care of my Mother, treat her as best you can, better than you would me." But to enjoin his Mother—and what a Mother!—that she take care of John, that would not only be superfluous but also insensitive. Gechter explains this very well:

> To call explicitly on Mary to take care of John with a mother's heart would have been not only unnecessary, but even indelicate.

Every woman with a normal sensitivity would understand this and would not have needed to be told, and much less if it were said by a dying son.[10]

❖

In the Palestine of those days, as also in ours, there existed a family custom of an almost sacred nature. When a woman was left alone, in the absence of a husband or sons, she would automatically be entrusted to the care of her own family, in the broad sense of the word: the relatives, the clan.

Given this invariable custom, in Mary's case, being without husband and children, it would have been natural for Jesus to entrust his Mother to the care of the Zebedee family—for example, to the care of Clopas, the husband of the Mary who was called the "sister" (cousin) of Mary (cf. Jn 19:25) and who was also at the foot of the cross. Or, as a last resort, to the older Zebedees, since the Jews were very sensitive to rights deriving from seniority.

In view of these same customs, the responsibility which Jesus was putting on John must have seemed very strange, if another sense were not discernible. The fact that those who were near the cross did not find Jesus' action strange as a testamentary disposition indicates that they perceived it was more than a juridical formality.

❖

As an aside, we are confronted here with a formidable indirect argument in favor of the perpetual virginity of Mary.

If Mary had had other sons, it would have been absurd, juridically and emotionally, to entrust Mary to the care of a stranger, establishing besides, maternal and filial bonds between them.

This is an incontestable fact which needs no further clarification.

❖

If Jesus' sole concern was to commit to John the temporal care of Mary, how can we explain the fact that the first to be addressed was Mary? If that mission and responsibility belonged to John, he should have been commissioned first.

What is most important is said first. Jesus established first the descending relation, enjoining Mary to take care of John like a son. From this fact it follows clearly that, in this double relationship, human concerns were not the issue and had no importance. It made no sense for Mary to take care of John; another more transcendental relationship existed.

> We must admit that in the new relationship of Mother and son, Mary fulfills the principal role, not John; and that the relationship which in the future will unite her to John, has its starting point in herself as in the case of every mother with regard to her son.[11]

We are interpreting the words of Jesus in the sense that the Lord wished to express a special attention toward his Mother by addressing her with words of consolation. But if this was the exclusive intention of Jesus, why did he speak an identical parallel commission to John? It seems strange that he would seek to console both John, as special as John may have been, and his own Mother with the same words.

Finally, as we have noted before, if Mary was entrusted to John, so was John entrusted to Mary. In other words, as John had to look after Mary, so in the same way, Mary had to look after John. That sounds very strange, because it so happened that the mother of John, Mary Salome, was also present. It would have been a direct offense to her. The context of this scene, therefore, indicates that the parallel words contain a much richer depth than its direct sense seems to manifest.

We Have a Mother

This series of precisions brings us to the conclusion that Jesus, in the present scene, is handing over his Mother to humanity.

What does "messianic" mean? It means that events or words do not end in themselves; they are not exhausted by their direct, natural or literal sense; rather they encompass a transcendent meaning and, in addition, refer to all people: transcendent and universal.

❖

Jesus had arrived at his "hour," at the culminating moment of his messianic role. His actions would correspond to the height of his destiny and the solemnity of the moment. Thus, the Lord Jesus, even though he was under the shock of a desperate physical situation, maintained his unalterable decision to fulfill the will of his Father, carrying out every disposition and leaving nothing undone.

After Jesus had established the relationship between Mary and John, the evangelist adds significantly: "After this, [Jesus was] aware that everything was now finished..." (Jn 19:28). These words indicate that, in the opinion of the evangelist, Jesus was conscious of having reached the climax of his messianic task, precisely and immediately after the episode involving Mary and John.

Hence we can conclude that the disposition of Jesus (Jn 19:25-28) has a messianic nature: in this mission Jesus entrusts humanity to Mary, as Mother, in the person of John. We conclude also that the testamentary gift of Mary to humanity, on the part of Jesus, was the final messianic act before he felt that all had been dutifully fulfilled.

❖

How can we explain the scope of the magnificent gift which Jesus in his last hour offers to humanity?

To have an exact understanding we must first say that the scene and the words—"Behold, your son," "Behold, your mother"—are somewhat similar to sacramental signs: they signify something and produce that which they signify.

Because of this Jesus brings about a concrete and sensible fact and establishes a juridical bond: John will consider Mary as his Mother and will offer her what a grown son should give his mother: affection and care. And Mary, in turn, will consider John as her son and will give him what a good mother always offers her son: attention and love.

This was the reality, the sign we would say, that Jesus brought about. But everything does not end here. On the contrary, all begins here. This concrete "gesture" contains, hidden and pulsating, one intention: to open its powerful meaning and spread it over an endless perspective of time and universality.

In John, the Lord was giving Mary as Mother to everyone in a supernatural, messianic sense. And reciprocally, Jesus Christ, in the present episode, declared and made all of the redeemed, children of Mary.

Thus, Christ was not primarily interested in creating a contract of civil rights between Mary and John but in beginning and developing between them a relationship of mother and son. Transcending the personal situation, Christ wishes to begin and develop existential and affective relationships between Mary and...who? According to the meaning of the word *messianic*, between Mary and all persons redeemed by his redemptive death on the cross. Gechter says:

> Given the fact that the Mother is one, but the children many, it remains sufficiently clear that in John are found represented all those whom Jesus wanted to redeem or all those who, in imitation of John, would believe in him.

From now on—forever—all of the redeemed have a Mother, by the explicit and ultimate will of the Lord; the very Mother of Jesus. Nobody in the world through the centuries would be left orphaned or alone on his journey through life. This interpretation satisfactorily exhausts the total significance of the text and context of John 19:25-28.

❖

Thus we understand why Jesus chose his most sensitive, loving disciple, John, for this meaningful mission. John would represent or symbolize in a perfect way the loving communication between a Mother and son. Thus we understand why Jesus entrusts his Mother to the care of the younger of Zebedee's sons and not to the elder as was customary, namely because of his tender and loving character.

This, in turn, indicates that Jesus wished to found a relationship based on reciprocal love: such it was between John and Mary; such it must and would be between believers and Mary. The relationship between the redeemed and the Mother would have to be carried out as mother-to-son. Now we also understand why the

Lord did not entrust his Mother to the care of his clan or family, or to the care of Salome, or to that group of women who would have received her with veneration and love, but, contrary to all custom, to the care of John.

We understand another detail also. Looking after parents was a primordial obligation of the Decalogue. Why did Christ delay in looking after his Mother's destiny until his last moments? He knew what was going to happen to him; one who was being crucified could scarcely speak. Why did he not dictate beforehand the arrangements pertaining to the future of his Mother?

Evidently Christ harbored within himself a special intention: to profit from the occasion to carry out the normal obligations of a son toward his mother and so establish a new ecclesial situation. Surely, Gechter says, Jesus included the fulfillment of his filial duties in his messianic task. This he accomplished by expressing through these duties a symbolic messianic content. Thus, and only thus, can we justify why Jesus delayed this care for his Mother until he could hardly speak. We must interpret this literally because immediately after, aware that all had been accomplished, he bowed his head and died.

This was his last will, his most cherished gift, the very best, at the end. In his last action he handed his Mother over to the Church, so that she would look after the Church with her maternal care and guide her on the way of salvation.

"Woman"

Unexpectedly, Jesus intentionally breaks the parallelism proper to the formulation of his spiritual testament. The concept of "son" corresponds to that of "mother." Addressing himself to Mary he should have done so with the word "Mother," not necessarily because his Mother was involved, but for the logical combination of mother-son involved in this scene.

The Aramean word for mother, *"imma,"* had a very intimate sense, equivalent to our expression "mama." Jesus substituted the word "woman" for the word "mother," in a context where logically we would expect the word "mama." Evidently it was a deliberate substitution. Why did he do so?

❖

One group of interpreters thinks that, with this change, Jesus acted with a unique sensitivity toward his Mother. To be the mother of one who was crucified was surely not a glorious honor—quite the contrary. To identify his Mother in these circumstances would have been a regrettable procedure. Calling her by the title "woman," Jesus wanted to draw the attention of the Sanhedrin, the executioners and the curious who were on the scene, away from the identity of his friends and relatives. In this way, no one would be able to identify the Mother of the crucified One.

But there was much more to it than that. The expression was chosen deliberately for a solemn moment and purpose.

In the messianic context of Calvary, the conceptual word "woman" takes Mary from a limited motherly function and opens to her an unlimited maternal destiny like the passage or crossing that we talked about in a previous chapter: from an exclusive and closed maternity according to the flesh to another maternity in faith, a universal and messianic one. In the present case Jesus ignores his identity as her Son, just as he did in other moments of his life.

As a true gentleman, and not lacking in affection, he gave the title "woman" to the Samaritan woman (cf. Jn 4:21), to Mary of Magdala (cf. Jn 20:15), to the Canaanite woman (cf. Mt 15:28) and to others. But for Christ to call the Samaritan or the Canaanite "woman" is not the same as calling his own Mother "woman." For that reason this expression has a different and messianic objective.

The word "woman" here is an immense evocation, combined and intermingled, of various scenes, persons and moments of salvation history. Seemingly, in the mind of the evangelist there was present the woman Eve, "mother of the living." Now this other woman (cf. Gen 3:15) is also present, who, through her offspring, will unmask the lies of the enemy. The woman of Revelation, whose Son will kill the dragon, is present. So also the Daughter of Zion, the first type of all those redeemed from captivity: And present is that other "woman" of the future, the Church who, like Mary, is also Virgin and Mother.

The "Woman" of Calvary assumes, summarizes and expresses all of these figures. She is the true "Mother of the living," the soil in which germinates the "firstborn among many brothers" (Rom 8:29), the inexhaustible fountain from which the people of the redeemed are born. All is summarized here and now in the fact that Mary receives children to whom she did not give birth, and Christ gives to her as children all of his disciples in the person of John.

The Exile

Countless times the same question has been asked: What is man? This question has the danger of involving us in never ending speculative philosophy. There is another, more concrete question: What does *feeling* human consist in? How is it experienced?

The precise answer: It is feeling like an exile.

❖

Animals *feel* they are in full harmony with nature by means of a totality of instinctive energies in tune with life. They live joyfully submerged "in" nature as in a home, in a deep and living "unity" with other beings. They feel themselves fully *realized*, although they are not conscious of it. They never experience dissatisfaction. They know nothing of frustration or boredom.

The human being is experientially conscious of himself.

When we first became conscious of ourselves, we began to feel solitary, as if expelled from the family which was our original unity with Life. Even if we are *part* of creation, we are in fact *apart* from creation. We share creation as though it were a home *alongside* other beings, but not *with* them: for at the same time we feel *outside* of the home, exiled and solitary.

And not only do we feel *outside* of creation, but also *above* creation: we feel superior to, and in a certain sense an enemy of, the creatures since we dominate and use them. We feel that we are lord, but an exiled lord, without a home, without a country.

Being conscious of ourselves, we are aware of and measure our own limitations, powerlessness and possibilities. This awareness of our limitations disturbs our interior peace, that joyous harmony experienced by other beings which are much lower on the scale of life than we are. Comparing our possibilities with our weaknesses, we begin to feel anxious. Anxiety leads us to frustration. Frustration launches us on an eternal path for the conquest of new roads, new frontiers.

Reason, says Fromm, is for us both a blessing and a curse.

❖

On the moral and spiritual level we feel ourselves more powerless than in any other field. Due to the feeling of solitude and exile, *egoism* was born and has grown like a leafy tree with thousands of large branches, which are our innumerable weapons of self-defense. Egoism has transformed the human being into a more solitary and sad being.

A most varied and tremendously complex web of biochemical and endocrinal elements condition our spontaneity—sometimes almost annulling our liberty—to the point that often "we do what we do not want to do, and that which we want to do we cannot do" (cf. Rom 7:14-25). We are thus prisoners.

Egoism—rather egocentrism—is in its origin a defensive weapon. It leads us to transform ourselves into a solitary castle, protected by walls, towers and escape routes. From the defensive we jump rapidly to the offensive, to conquest and domination.

The definitive destiny of the human being in the progressive evolution of history is to vanquish egoism: even more, it is to free the person's great energies, chained today to his own ego, and to launch them for the service of all, a service of kindness and love.

The human being is therefore imprisoned, an expatriate and alone, in need of a Redeemer, a Country and a Mother.

Consolation

To counter the feeling of exile and solitude we need to feel Someone near us. In the Bible our God is always presented as a Person, loving and loved, who is "with us," especially on desolate days. This is the melody that rings throughout the Bible, from the first page to the last: "Do not fear. I am with you."

This melody raises its tone in the prophets and the voice of God is transformed into an immense choir with phrases like these: "I will not leave you nor forsake you. ...Be firm and steadfast! ...for the LORD, your God, is with you wherever you go" (Jos 1:5, 9).

We hear expressions like these: "Do not distrust me, for I am your God. I am protecting you with my victorious right hand. I am taking you by the hand and telling you: 'Do not be afraid.' If you cross a river, the current will not carry you away. If you pass through the midst of flames, you will not burn. Do not look to the past but to the future, because there you will see prodigies: rivers will run on barren hills, fountains will gush in deserts and springtime flourish in the steppes. All this and much more will happen so that all may know and understand that it is the Holy One of Israel who is the author of such marvels" (cf. Is 41; 43).

❖

Frequently the voice of God changes into the tenderness of the Father: "I thought about you when you were still in your mother's womb. I have loved you with an eternal love. Israel, when you were still a small child, I took you up in my arms, I fed you, and lifted you close to my cheek" (cf. Jer 31; Hos 11).

Jesus emphasizes still more the care and tenderness of the Father. He declares to us that *Father* is the new name of God. With deep emotion he tells us that our first obligation does not consist in loving God but in letting ourselves be loved by God.

In a symphony of comparisons, metaphors and parables, he tells us things immensely consoling: at times the Father takes the form of a shepherd, climbs the mountains, shows himself on the cliffs and runs into the valleys to look for a lost and dear son. When the son returns home, the Father prepares a great feast. The Father waits—hoping for the return of the ungrateful and reckless son who has run away from home. His mercy is much greater than our sins and his love very much greater than our solitude. If the Father takes care to clothe the flowers and feed the sparrows, how much more will he take care of our needs!

❖

But it was not enough to have a father. In life—in all life—there is a father and a mother. Rather, a mother and a father. Psychiatry tells us about the decisive influence of the mother on each of us, before and after birth; and also about the dangers of that influence in the case of fixations and dependencies. All of us preserve, especially from the early years of our childhood, memories of this mother who was for us a stimulator and consoler.

This is why Jesus Christ revealed the Father to us and gifted us with a Mother.

As we explained above, Jesus Christ entrusted his Mother to humanity so that humanity could take care of her with faith and veneration, and he entrusted humanity to Mary so that she could take care of us and transform us into a kingdom of love.

But humanity does not exist concretely; people exist—or better yet, each person exists. Therefore Jesus, a great pedagogue, made a gift of his Mother to the concrete person of John as a representative of humanity. With this symbolic act Jesus wished to signify that, as the mother-son relationship of Mary and John developed in mutual care, in the same way the relationship of the redeemed with Mary must develop.

❖

Christian people, during long periods of time, have shown Mary a filial affection, starting from situations of need such as exile, abandonment, solitude; thus was born that immense prayer of supplication, the "Hail, Holy Queen." For many centuries the "Hail, Holy Queen" has been the unique morning star, lighthouse of hope, prayer of salvation for millions of people in disasters, agonies, temptations and the struggles of life.

Would it not be a danger to turn our Mother Mary into the alienating maternal womb about which certain psychiatry speaks? It is evident for those psychiatrists for whom only "matter" exists, that salvation consists in accepting our radical solitude, in drawing away from any "mother" and in standing on our own feet by our own power. Some program!

As for us, we live in a world of faith: redeemed by Jesus Christ who died and rose, embraced by the strong and loving arms of God the Father, and cared for by a consoling Mother given to us by Jesus in his last hour on earth. Many psychiatrists are in another world and will never understand the "things" of the faith. They will affirm that alienation is everywhere. It makes sense for them to say so.

❖

Sometimes a person is assaulted by desolation and does not know why. The confessions of men or women who come to us and speak openly are simply overwhelming. They say that they do not know what it is. It is about something interior which is confusing, complex, absolutely inexplicable, something which brings them a heavy sadness from which escape seems impossible. They add that in these moments the one way to be relieved is to have recourse to Mary, saying: "Our life, our sweetness and our hope, turn your eyes of mercy toward us!"

They always say that it is impossible to explain: some days they wake up and, without any apparent reason, they begin to feel a vague and deep impression of terror. They feel pessimistic, as though rejected by everyone. Of a hundred memories, ninety-five of which are positive, their imagination will focus on the five negative ones, and they are overpowered by a strange sense of sadness, fear and shock that they cannot run away from. Without knowing why, they wish they could die. But they add that in these moments only the memory of their heavenly Mother, with the words of the "Hail, Holy Queen" relieves them, that their courage returns and they begin to breathe again.

❖

During my long life I have helped many persons at the hour of their last agony. I still remember many of these cases. When an agonizing person, in spite of the many vain words of relatives, feels drawn by the inexorable law of death, how often have I seen his or her face light up at the recitation of the "Hail, Holy Queen": "To you we cry, poor banished children of Eve; to you we send up our sighs, Mother of mercy and sweetness."

In countries of Catholic tradition, one is frequently impressed by the depth of Marian devotion among the sailors and fishermen. In many places, when the boats leave for the high seas they always do so with the singing of the "Hail, Holy Queen." In the villages of these fishermen the people never tire of telling stories about impossible situations solved by Mary, of entire fleets saved by one "Hail, Holy Queen."

❖

But we are not sailors or fishermen, though we are sailors on the sea of life. Undoubtedly life is a struggle and frequently ends in failure. Alas for the one who fails; he will be alone, and from the fallen tree everybody will want to cut some wood. Who among us has not experienced the consolation of a mother in the time of failure? The mother is courage before the combat and consolation in failure.

I have seen prisoners stigmatized by public opinion, abandoned by all their relatives and friends, but visited by a discreet and lonely woman, their own mother. A mother never abandons, if she is not herself taken away by death.

We need another Mother, one who will never be the victim of death. Each one of us lives our life in a unique way, and we alone "know" about our own "archives;" we endure difficulties, enter into desolations, our state of mind has its ups and downs, hopes die; suddenly we are surrounded by impossible situations. The following day hope recovers and, though with difficulty, everything seems to work out all right. Such is the struggle of life!

Mary is consolation and peace in every moment. She transforms what is rough to sweetness, the struggle to calm; she is benign and gentle. She suffers with those who suffer, waits with those who wait and departs with those who depart. The Mother is patience and security. She is our joy, our delight and our rest. The Mother is an immense sweetness and an invincible fortress.

CHAPTER 13

Between Combat and Hope

Alienation and Reality

Everything in us that does not open us outward is egoism. Marian devotion which turns in on oneself is false and alienating. An association with Mary which searches exclusively for security or consolation without moving outward toward the construction of a kingdom of love is not only subtle self-seeking but a danger to the normal development of the personality.

No doubt in many places, in the long run, Marian devotion has resulted in a paralysis of energies. Medals and scapulars, for many people, have been magic amulets rather than evocations of a dynamic Mother. Many have looked for images and pictures, something to touch and kiss, instead of seeking signs which awaken faith and lead to loving.

It certainly is not always this way. Nor should we make caricatures and generalize. Often it boils down to a kind of mixture of superstition, interest and true devotion.

Great multitudes approach Marian shrines with a minimum of good sentiments and an element of personal interest. They wish to receive something or give thanks for a favor. At times we have the impression that we are witnessing a sales transaction. This is the case with so many faithful who make touching sacrifices like walking long distances on foot, crawling on one's knees or lighting candles; in spite of devotional appearances these persons often hide a good dose of egoistic interest. They fulfill what the old Romans used to say: *"do ut des,"* "I give so that you may give." Hence, in some Latin countries there is a custom called "paying the token." The word "pay" carries the clear concept of a purchase and sales agreement.

Today it is about the health of a mother, tomorrow the acceptance of a son into the university, the next day a good husband for the daughter, another day, a marriage, family or neighborhood conflict. The bottom line is really a search for themselves; they do not seek to love. Very rarely will they ask for another set of values such as faith, humility and courage.

It is evident that all of this is an adulteration of the reason Jesus Christ entrusted us to a Mother. Instead of a Mother who forms Jesus in us, we often want to make of her a financier who solves our economic setbacks, a doctor who heals our incurable illnesses, a magician who has the secret formula for all our impossible situations.

Other persons hasten to Marian shrines because they have heard of miracles; they go with a mixture of curiosity, superstition and fascination. Unknowingly, instead of increasing in faith, they risk stirring up religious emotions. Naturally, such feelings are not the same as real faith.

❖

Alienation can come from another angle. Among experts, Mary has historically been the object of partisan rivalries between those called "maximalists" and "minimalists." Both of these groups claim to know the *real* Mary. Both would carry their position to its extreme and caricature their doctrinal adversaries.

Vatican Council II was an impressive example of how the Marian theme is laden with high emotional tension. It is an incredible paradox that this woman could be the center of polemic, she who in the Gospel always appears in a secondary role, scarcely opening her mouth, full of calm.

Pretending to exalt Mary by presenting her life as a little less than a continual enjoyment of the beatific vision is stealing from her the merit and condition of a pilgrim of faith—alienating her. Such excessively deductive mariology runs the danger of lifting Mary to triumphalist heights, surrounding her with unlimited privileges and prerogatives. There are some who place Mary so high and so distant that they transform her into a dehumanized demi-goddess.

> This creature "blessed among all women" was on this earth a humble woman, committed to the condition of privation, work, oppression and the uncertainty of tomorrow which are the lot of underdeveloped countries.
>
> Mary did not only have to wash and fold the clothing but to sew it; not only to sew but, before that, to weave it.
>
> She did not only have to make bread but also to grind the grain, and to cut wood for the needs of the home, as the women in Nazareth still do.
>
> The Mother of God was not a queen like those on earth but a spouse and a mother of laborers. She was not rich but poor.
>
> It was necessary that the "Theotokos" [Mother of God] be the Mother of one condemned to die under

the triple condemnation of popular hostility and of the religious and civil authorities of his country. It was necessary for her to share with him the working and oppressed condition which was that of the mass of people whom he had to redeem, "those who labor and are burdened."[12]

Mary is not sovereign but rather a servant. She is not the goal, but rather the way. She is not a demi-goddess but the Poor One of God. She is not all-powerful but an intercessor. She is above all the Mother who continues to give birth to Jesus Christ in us.

Our Maternal Destiny

The profound meaning of spiritual motherhood consists in this, that Mary again be the Mother of Jesus *"in us."* Every mother is pregnant and gives birth. The Mother of Christ is pregnant with and gives birth to Christ. Spiritual motherhood means that Mary is pregnant with Christ and gives birth to him "in" us and "through" us.

In a word, the birth of Christ means that we *incarnate* and "give birth" to the *existential Christ*—allow me the expression—to the very same Christ who felt, acted and lived in his human existence. Jesus Christ—the Church—is born and grows in the measure that the attitudes and behavior, reactions and style of Christ *"appear through"* our lives.

Therefore, we have a "maternal" vocation to "be pregnant with" and "give birth" to Jesus Christ. The Church "is" Jesus Christ. The growth of the Church is proportionate to the growth of Christ. But the total Christ does not grow by juxtaposition. In other words, the Church is not "greater" because we have so many institutions, so many mission centers or catechetical sessions.

The Church has an internal dimension which is very easily overlooked. The Church is the Body of Christ or the complete Christ. She grows from within, by interior assimilation. When contemplated in depth, she cannot be reduced to statistics or mathematical proportions: for example, the Church is not "greater" because we have celebrated seven hundred marriages and two thousand baptisms. The Church is the complete Christ. And Jesus Christ grows in the measure that we reproduce his life in ourselves.

In the measure that we incarnate the conduct and attitudes of Christ, the complete Christ advances toward his fullness. It is especially with our lives, more than with our institutions, that we impel Christ to a constant growth. God has not called us from all eternity to transform the world with efficiency and organization, but "to be conformed to the image of his Son" (Rom 8:29).

❖

Mary will give birth to Christ *in us* in the measure that we are *sensitive*, like Christ, to all the needs of this world; in the measure that we live like that Christ who sympathized and identified himself with another's misfortune, who could not witness an affliction without being touched, who stopped eating or resting to attend to a sick person, who not only felt sorry but found solutions. Mary is the Mother who must help us to *incarnate* this living Christ, suffering with those who suffer, so that we ourselves live for others and not for ourselves.

❖

Mary gives birth to Christ in us in the measure that the *poor* are our *favorites;* when the poor of this world are looked after with preference, this will be the sign that we are in the truly messianic Church; when we live like Christ with hands and heart open to the poor, with a visible sympathy for them, sharing their condition and solving their problems; in the measure that our activity is preferentially, though not exclusively, dedicated to them; in the measure that we come to them with hope and without resentment. Mary will be truly Mother in the measure that we allow her to incarnate in us this Christ of the poor.

❖

Mary will give birth to Christ in us in the measure that we try to be like Jesus, humble and patient; in the measure that we reflect his state of mind, of peace, of self-mastery, of courage and serenity; when we act as Jesus did before judges and accusers with silence, patience and dignity; when we forgive as he forgave; when we keep silent as he kept silent; when we are not interested in our own glory but in the glory of the Father and the happiness of our brothers and sisters; when we know how to risk our lives, behaving with courage and boldness like Christ; when we have the interests of the Father and of our brothers and sisters at heart; when we are sincere and truthful before enemies and friends as Jesus was, defending the truth even at the cost of our lives. Mary will truly be our Mother in the measure that we let her incarnate in us this poor and humble Christ.

❖

Mary will give birth to Christ in us in the measure that we are *disinterested* in ourselves and *concerned* about others, like Jesus who never thought of himself, forgetting to eat, sleep and rest; in the measure that we sacrifice ourselves like Christ, without groaning, without murmuring, without bitterness, without threats, at the same time giving hope and courage to others; in the measure that we love as Christ did, inventing a thousand ways and means to express that love, surrendering his life and prestige for his friends; if we pass through life, like Jesus, "doing good to all." In what does the spiritual motherhood of Mary consist? It consists in Mary helping us to incarnate, to be pregnant with and to give birth to Jesus who loved to the utmost.

❖

Mary will be for us the true Mother if we strive to imitate her *fraternal kindness:* immediately after the annunciation she hurried to congratulate Elizabeth and helped her with the domestic tasks in preparation for the birth. She will be our true Mother if we imitate the delicate and attentive concern she showed for all those present at Cana, as though they were members of her own family; her supreme delicacy in not mentioning the lack of wine to anyone, in not informing the host, so as to avoid his being humiliated, and a greater delicacy yet— her hope to save the situation herself without anyone becoming aware of the problem; delicate also with regard to her own Son as she avoids letting anyone suspect that there was a misunderstanding between Jesus and herself by telling the servants: "Do whatever he tells you to do" (Jn 2:5). We see her delicacy in Capernaum when, instead of entering the house to greet her Son with a sort of maternal pride, she knocks at the door and remains outside, hoping to be received by the Son.

In this manner Mary gives birth to Christ through us, we in turn fulfill our maternal vocation, and Christ is "greater" than ever.

CHAPTER 14

Conclusion

The Transhistorical Journey and Consummation

We are the builders of a kingdom. Our worst enemy is impatience. A project of eternal dimensions, we would like to see the kingdom completed in our lifetime. We need wisdom to measure our limitations and the dimensions of this project. The weapons of wisdom are patience and hope.

We were born yesterday and we have millions of years ahead of us. Our earth and our history will not end in an apocalyptic upheaval but by a normal cosmogenic extinction.

For thousands of years, there was nothing but an enormous, formless mass of cosmic gas. This gas formed a gigantic molecule which, when it exploded, organized nebulae, galaxies and solar systems which are nothing but particles of the explosion. By force of gravity, which tends to unite bodies, the cosmic dust flowing from this explosion began to concentrate in circular systems around a principal center. This is the theory of cosmogenesis, based on mathematical principles, and the theory of "the universe in expansion."

What awaits humanity? We must look to the past so as to foresee what will happen in the future. The chemical constitution of the universe is extraordinarily uniform. The stars are but the thermonuclear reactions of the universe through which hydrogen is transformed into helium. The stars are transformed into irradiations of light, heat and molecules. The life of our galaxies, and consequently of our sun and earth is calculated to last for some five billion years.

The earth was rich in inorganic substances. Life sprang up as an effect of the organization of these substances, through the union of combined elements. Life began in the sea, approximately two billion years ago.

Once life was born, it reproduced and multiplied itself in multicellular beings. With the passing of millions of years species were formed with nervous and cerebral systems.

Then after more millions of years, in "the end times," the process of *"hominization"* (let us call it that) happened through an accelerated cerebral complication. The first traces of the history of civilization appeared, according to the present theory of paleontology, around seven thousand years ago with the Sumerians. Abraham lived less than four thousand years ago.

The conclusion: we were born yesterday. Jesus Christ took flesh at the beginning of the history of humanity.

❖

What does Christ attempt to do in this broad expanse of history?

The task of Jesus Christ is to transform the world, or more exactly, to transform the heart of the person. The stupendous project, conceived and dreamt up by God from eternity and carried out "in time" by Jesus Christ, is the *divinization* of the human being.

God created us in his image and likeness. The Lord deposited in our hearts a divine seed which impels us not to become "god," as a substitute for the true God (cf. Gen 3:5), but to become "divine," sharing in the divine nature. Having created us in the beginning similar to him, his subsequent plans have been to make us more similar to him.

❖

We have just recently "come out of the woods." Because of this, in this evolving phase of humanity, we are still dominated, governed and organized entirely by the instinctive mechanisms of our egoism. For the inferior beings on the scale of life, the reactive instincts are essentially egocentric so as to defend themselves and survive in the struggle for life. From these we too draw our congenital egoistical nature. Even today, the human being is *connaturally* egoistical.

The Bible does not tire of telling us in a thousand ways that egoism (sin) reaches the very roots of the human being; or, said in another way, the human being is structurally "in sin," in egoism (cf. Ps 51; Rom 7:14-25). From this structure of sin emerge all the fruits of the "flesh": fornication, impurity, debauchery, idolatry, sorcery, hatred, discord, envy, anger, resentment, division, dissension, jealousy, drunkenness, orgies and the like (cf. Gal 5:19-22).

The gigantic and transhistorical task of Jesus Christ consists in having us "pass" out of the laws of egoism. And since God "is" love, our divinization will consist in "passing" from egoism to love, in ceasing to be "human" to become like God.

❖

I dare say that redemption has cosmic dimensions, which is what remains to be explained. Due to our egoistical nature, we dominate and "submit to our vanity" (cf. Rom 8:20) all creatures. These, submitted to our arbitrary and despotic whim, feel like tortured prisoners, and moan (cf. Rom 8:22), yearning to be liberated from that oppression.

To describe this profound phenomenon, St. Francis used the word *"appropriate."* To have is one thing, to ʳᵉtain is another. To use is different from appropriation, ˟ve it all for ourselves. To appropriate means to at-
put a chain between us and a creature, between proprietor and property. A terrible mystery and a deep ignorance: the human being believes that to be "lord" consists in having the maximum number of appropriations, when in reality, the contrary is true. The more possessions we have, the more attached we are, the more chains enslave us to creatures, because they cry out for their master, as the Romans said, *"res clamat domino,"* "the thing cries out for its lord."

The poorest person in the world is the freest person in the world, and consequently more lord. Our redemption, our liberation, comes through disappropriation. Poverty and love are one and the same thing.

Paul tells us that creatures are sighing to be liberated from the abuse of human beings. If we *"detach ourselves"* from creatures such as human values, charisms, goods, if we do not use them in a domineering way, these creatures remain free. Our liberation therefore constitutes the liberation of creatures. That is, creatures are free from us when we detach ourselves from them.

Now, if we do not subject creatures to our exclusive

gain, these then can be handed over to the service of others. Thus, human energies and values, once liberated from abuse, can now enter into the realm of love, since they are left free and available for the service of all our brothers and sisters.

Entering into the sphere of love, both human beings and creatures remain within the process of *divinization*, because God is Love. They are free to serve and to love.

❖

This prodigious and slow paschal liberation will happen through the redemptive grace of Jesus Christ. The Vatican Council says: "The key, the center, and the goal of all history is found in its Master and Lord Jesus Christ." In other words, not only is Jesus Christ in the heart of history, but the paschal movement of history is impelled and advanced by the dynamic redemption of the Lord. The *raison d'être* of human history is to liberate the great human energies, today fastened to the egocentric rings of the human being, and to pour them out in the service of all peoples.

Naturally, this is a thousand years' task. In this liberation, earthly processes and realities will effectively help us in our journey toward liberation and love. Thus, for example, democratic and socializing movements, it seems to me, will prove to be a great help in this process, in the measure that they ensure mutual respect, oppose individualism, and open up human beings, beyond sovereignties, countries and frontiers, to the universality of an integrated fellowship.

It is evident that, in this transhistorical redemption, human sciences such as psychology, medicine, sociology and technical knowledge will play a precious role. The Council affirms that in this progress toward liberty and love we will meet many enemies such as sickness, injustice, poverty, ignorance. Science and technology will assist us in defeating these enemies.

According to *Gaudium et Spes*, technology is the great victory of humanity over the inexorable forces of nature. Yet, according to the conciliar text, this liberating technology is bringing us into another slavery, because of the imbalance and ambivalence it produces (cf. GS 8, 9, 10). And the Council challenges us to conquer these negative ambivalences.

The Church nourishes an immense hope that we will finally overcome all the obstacles, because we are marked in the depth of our hearts with the image of God. We carry within ourselves the immortal cells capable of healing all errors, overcoming all difficulties and walking unceasingly onward and upward.

But in this triumphal march there will always remain *"the" enemy:* sin. The Council ends by asking itself and by challenging us to see how, beyond earthly and human victories, we can arrive at transforming our egocentric vital energies into love. More simply, how can we manage to fight, suffer and work for others' interests with the same enthusiasm we have for our own interests?

❖

The optimism of the Church moves on to other terrain: we will also conquer sin because there is Someone who has already defeated it—Jesus Christ. "The truth is that only in the mystery of the incarnate Word does the mystery of man take on light" (GS 22).

In the measure that human beings, over the duration of millennia, progress in assuming and incarnating the values and attitudes of Jesus—in that measure will the consequences of egoism progressively disappear: violence, injustice, war, discrimination and exploitation.

In the measure that more people assume more deeply the "extreme love" of Jesus (cf. Jn 13:1) and become capable of "giving their life" (Jn 15:18) for their brothers and sisters, will liberating redemption advance slowly but surely through the narrow paths of history and reach the *"superhumanism"* through which and in which freedom and love will shine in all their splendor.

More millennia will pass. And, in the measure that people resemble Jesus more, will humanity go on *"christifying itself,"* Jesus Christ will go on *growing* to the adult stature that should be his.

More and more the kingdom will be one of freedom and love, and people will be ever more fulfilled and happy, until egoism is definitively suppressed from the human heart; the great human psychic energies will not be directed to each one's center but toward others; we will love one another as Jesus loved us; Christ will *truly* "live" in us, each one and all will "be" Christ. This will be *the end,* and the curtain of history will come down.

God will be "all in all" and Jesus Christ will have reached his perfect fullness. Read the Letters to the Colossians and to the Ephesians.

The conclusion of the Council is magnificent and sublime: "...the ultimate vocation of man is in fact one, and divine" (GS 22).

❖

It is evident that, in this birth and growth of Christ through history, the same Mother who brought him into this world will play a predominant role.

Mary will preside over this process, and not only will she preside but she will be the fundamental Mother of this entire divinizing and liberating transformation, through us, her redeemed children.

❖

This process will be a task of long millennia. We know exactly when our planet will be "uninhabitable": when there will no longer be conditions for life on earth because of the death of the sun.

The sun "lives" and enables us to live by its light and heat through the transformation of hydrogen to helium, brought about by thermonuclear reactions. Science knows how many tons of hydrogen our king star, the sun, consumes each second. It knows also how much hydrogen the sun has left. We can therefore calculate perfectly the time the sun will need to consume this amount. When all of this combustible substance is exhausted, the sun will agonize and die, and there will be no more possibility of life on earth.

Thus, humanity has millions of years before it to attain its *christification.*

❖

People of Jesus Christ are the collaborators alongside Mary in this transcendental task. Our danger is to allow ourselves to be carried away by impatience, due to *"temporality,"* that is, feeling ourselves submerged "in" time, as in the thought of Heidegger. We feel in a hurry to solve everything urgently, because we have the impression that the destiny of the world will be decided during the course of our own lifetime.

We do not know how to situate ourselves in the perspective of faith. It is sufficient that, for the duration of our existence, we place our brick in the building of the kingdom of liberty and love. This "brick" will remain there, irremovable, forever and ever.

When we die, unbreakable silence and eternal oblivion will fall upon us. But if we have given an impulse to Jesus Christ in his growth, we will have inscribed an indelible mark in history which neither silence nor oblivion will ever erase, and our name will always remain written among the number of the chosen ones.

❖

This transhistorical transformation implies, as we have said, duties and temporal tasks. Right here the almost insuperable difficulty of discernment arises, and for people of the Gospel, the danger of *temporalism* begins again.

It is tremendously difficult to establish the dividing line between the contingency of politics and its transcendence. Concretely, what does a political commitment mean for a member of the clergy? To what limits can a priest go in political action? As for taking concrete steps, what do such expressions as solidarity, leadership, denunciation, liberation, prophetic stance mean?

In what do the temporal activities of a Christian lay person differ from that of a priest or a sister? Does such a difference exist? If it exists, what are its concrete implications? Up to what point can one advance? Where are the boundaries? We are surrounded by a dense fog.

We must call on the Spirit of Wisdom so that we will not be committed too little or too much.

❖

Of what worth is it to invoke God when the true "god" of this world is money? Is it of any help to call ourselves followers of Jesus Christ when the means we use and glory in are the exploitation of one another, domination over one another, and the pitiless competition for economic superiority?

What do we gain by declaring ourselves baptized if the only ideals we reflect are hedonism, the pride of life and the desire to stand out and shine? Children of the Gospel have nothing to look for in the kingdom of money.

What is the value of social revolution if people continue hating each other, if they cultivate ferocious ambitions and substitute the aristocracy of money for the aristocracy of intelligence?

If a social revolution destroys money and combats individualism, it has contributed to the transformation of humanity. But what do we do if the heart continues rotting, and in its wake is left a stream of bitterness?

❖

The heart of the human being does not change by an act of magic. Tearing down social structures and replacing them with others is relatively easy, because it is achieved by a rapid and spectacular action and consequently is rather fascinating.

But to bring down the barriers of egoism, to create a new heart, to purify the motives and criteria of human beings, to work for others with the same interest as if it were for ourselves, to not worry about ourselves but about others, to acquire the capacity of forgiving, of understanding—all this is a task for centuries and millennia. This is the great revolution of Jesus Christ.

The "world" believes that the last one to strike is the champion. "To whom can we compare this champion?" asked Jesus. A champion is one, answers Christ, who after being struck on the right cheek remains so entirely self-controlled that he can quietly offer the left. This person is the stronger of the two. What a revolution in that comparison alone!

❖

The results of a temporal action, I repeat, are, or can be, colorful and flashy, but also superficial, because they do not touch the heart. Generally speaking, that which is attained rapidly, rapidly wears out.

The Father entrusted Jesus with transforming the world and leading humanity, liberated and divinized, in a great movement back to the house of the Father. This is not a task of one century or of a millennium. Jesus Christ is yesterday, today, tomorrow and always. It is necessary that the followers of Jesus Christ, his collaborators in the construction of his kingdom, position themselves "in the time" of Jesus Christ, not losing sight of the dimensions of faith.

We must not become impatient, looking for immediate results. We must know how to discern what is the Gospel and what is not; and above all, we need to have, like the prophets, our roots sunk deeply in an intimacy with the Lord.

> The prophet is one possessed by God. But this is not why he has withdrawn from the world.
>
> Linked closely to his contemporaries he lives with intensity the events of his time.
>
> Witness of the absolute power of God, he is gifted with a sharp and acute gaze.
>
> Before him, façades crumble, humanity's machinations lose their spectacularity and their littleness appears openly.
>
> A fire penetrates him, an interior strength pushes him on; in season and out of season he must announce that for which he is responsible.
>
> He carries with him evidence of the presence of God and of the vision of God on the world, and he deeply

challenges the lack of insight of those around him. They would say that he is a seer who goes around in the kingdom of the blind.

For the prophet, truth comes from on high; to him it is given as something imposed on him, to which he cannot resist.[13]

It is necessary to organize a great liberation march in the interior of the human being.

❖

We are the children of hope, and hope is the soul of our combat. We form an immortal chain whose first and last link is the same One who has defeated egoism and death.

Hope is the favorite daughter of God. Failures will never discourage people of hope. After the first, the fifth, the twentieth and hundredth failure, hope always repeats the same thing: "It does not matter; tomorrow will be better." Hope never dies. It is immortal, like God himself.

Children of the Gospel shout: "It is impossible to defeat egoism." Hope replies: "All is possible for God." People of the Gospel murmur: "Money is an invincible machine." Hope responds: "Only God is invincible."

Children of the Gospel lose courage, crying out that money and hate rule the world and make fun of love; they say that hate belongs to the strong and love to the weak; they say also that it is preferable to be feared than loved; they say that to triumph it is necessary to lose all sense of guilt and that egoism is a serpent with a thousand heads which penetrates and sustains in a cold and impassive way the whole society of consumerism. In the face of all this, followers of the Gospel feel tempted to "leave" the world, saying: "There is no place for hope!"

Hope answers: "You, children of combat and of hope, you are mistaken, because you are looking downward. Everything appears to be lost, because you believe in statistics and read the newspapers; your faith is based on sociological surveys; you only believe in what you see.

"Lift up your eyes and look where the source of hope is: Jesus Christ, risen from the dead, conqueror of egoism and of sin. He is our only hope.

"Hope dies in you because you lean on the results of human projects. When the march of the Church is colorful and triumphant, when the clergy is numerous and the seminaries full, you say: 'Everything goes well.'

"When the Church is reduced to silence and her witnesses are imprisoned or decapitated, you say: 'All is lost.' The fountain of hope is not in statistics nor in the brightness of any phenomena. Have you forgotten the cross and the grain of wheat? Do you not know that the resurrection of the Lord was born in the death of the Lord? Remember: the crucifixion and the resurrection are one and the same thing.

"So as not to succumb to discouragement, in moments when results are not visible, rely on the Immortal One of all centuries. We are invincible because the Lord has vanquished all his enemies. The only ruler that remained on earth was death, and death was also conquered by the Immortal One."

> Then I saw the heavens opened, and there was a white horse; its rider was [called] "Faithful and True."
>
> His eyes were [like] a fiery flame, and on his head were many diadems.
>
> He wore a cloak that had been dipped in blood, and his name was called the Word of God. The armies of heaven followed him, mounted on white horses and wearing clean white linen.

> He has a name written on his cloak and on his thigh,
> "King of kings and Lord of lords."

> —*Revelation 19:11, 12, 13-14, 16*

Christ, with his Mother's collaboration and ours, will go on eradicating the roots of injustice; he will establish the foundations of peace, and the sun of justice will begin to shine.

The witnesses of Jesus Christ and children of his Mother will be obliged to take their responsibilities with the audacity of the Holy Spirit and with the equilibrium of God. And a new epoch will begin in which the poor will take their place in the kingdom, there will be liberation from all slavery, and dispersed energies will reunite. The children of the Father and of the Mother will form a unique and loving people. Mary will preside over this gradual operation. Many witnesses will fall; others will desert. But the kingdom will rise upward, stone by stone.

It will be a kingdom in which the spiritual and the temporal will be integrated with one another; one which will move beyond oppressive structures to the suppression of social calamities, to the acquisition of what is necessary, to the increase of dignity, to the promotion of peace and participation in decisions.

It will be a kingdom in which the family will be ruled by love and will be a school of formation for persons, where spouses will be witnesses of faith and cooperators of grace; the home will be the temple of God and a school of mutual respect.

It will be a kingdom where there will not be many who have little and a few who have much, inequalities will be levelled, lack of sensitivity toward others will cease, frustrations will disappear. The privileged and the forgotten, problems and tensions, the domination of some over others—none of these will exist.

It will be a kingdom of peace in which dignity will be respected, legitimate aspirations will be satisfied and the children of God will be the agents of their own destiny; a kingdom in which the children of God, in a dynamic process, will be the artisans of peace and, because of this, called blessed (cf. Mt 5:9). This peace will be the fruit of love and the sign of universal brotherhood.

> Then I saw a new heaven and a new earth. The former heaven and the former earth had passed away, and the sea was no more. I also saw the holy city, a new Jerusalem, coming down out of heaven from God, prepared as a bride adorned for her husband. I heard a loud voice from the throne saying, "Behold, God's dwelling is with the human race. He will dwell with them and they will be his people and God himself will always be with them [as their God]. He will wipe every tear from their eyes, and there shall be no more death or mourning, wailing or pain, [for] the old order has passed away."
>
> The one who sat on the throne said, "Behold, I make all things new."
>
> He said to me, "They are accomplished. I [am] the Alpha and the Omega, the beginning and the end.
>
> "...I shall be his God, and he will be my son."
>
> *—Revelation 21:1-5, 6, 7*

❖

Lady of silence and of the cross,
Lady of love and of surrender,
Lady of the word received
and of the word cherished,
Lady of peace and of hope,
Lady of all who journey,
because you are the Lady of the way of Easter.

We have also partaken of the bread of friendship and fraternal union. We feel strong and happy. Our sorrow will turn to joy, and our joy will be full, and no one will be able to take it from us.

Show us, Mary, the gratitude and joy of all detachments; teach us to say "Yes" always with all our soul. Enter into the fragility of our heart and pronounce, yourself, this "Yes" in our stead.

Be the way for those who die and the serenity of those who remain. Accompany us always while we are on pilgrimage together to the Father.

Teach us that this life is always a parting, always a detachment and an offering, always a transition and a paschal feast, until we reach the final transition and the definitive paschal celebration.

Then we shall understand that to live we need to die, to meet all together in the Lord we must part, and that we must pass through many limitations before entering into glory.

> Our Lady of reconciliation,
> image and principle of the Church:
> today we deposit in your heart,
> poor, silent and available,
> this Church on her pilgrimage to Easter.
>
> A Church essentially missionary,
> leaven and soul of the society in which we live,
> a prophetic Church which wants to announce
> that the kingdom has come.
>
> A Church of authentic witnesses
> inserted in the history of humanity
> as the saving presence of the Lord,
> fountain of peace, of joy and of hope. Amen.

—*Cardinal Pironio*

PART ONE

Chapter 1

[1] *Biblia de Jerusalén:* "Introduccíon."
[2] Paul Gechter, *María en el Evangelio,* Bilbao 1959, p. 40.
[3] Ibid., p. 40.
[4] Ibid., p. 40.
[5] Ibid., p. 104.
[6] Ibid., p. 100.
[7] Ibid., p. 91.
[8] Ibid., p. 103.
[9] Ibid., p. 108.

Chapter 2

[10] Karl Hermann Schelkle, *María, Madre del Redentor,* Barcelona 1965, p. 93.

PART TWO

Chapter 3

[1] See my book, *Muéstrame tu Rostro,* pp. 133-174.

Chapter 4

[2] K. H. Schelkle, *María, Madre del Redentor,* p. 74.
[3] Ibid., p. 76.

Chapter 5

[4] Ibid., p. 72.
[5] Ibid., p. 73.
[6] Ibid., p. 73.
[7] See my book, *Muéstrame tu Rostro,* pp. 438-446.

Chapter 6

[8] G. Ricciotti, *Vida de Jesucristo,* p. 259.

[9] Ibid., p. 259.

[10] Ibid., p. 259.

[11] Ibid., pp. 259, 260.

[12] F. William, *Vida de María,* p. 102.

[13] Ibid., p. 103.

[14] Ricciotti, *Vida de Jesucristo,* p. 250.

PART THREE

Chapter 8

[1] See my book, *Muéstrame tu Rostro,* the entire chapter "Contemplative Life."

[2] As regards customs, the meaning of the espousals, etc., refer to the expertise of the German exegete, Paul Gechter, *María en el Evangelio,* pp. 123-195.

[3] Ibid., p. 155.

Chapter 9

[4] Ibid., p. 202.

[5] Ibid., 217.

[6] Josef Schmid, *El Evangelio Según San Lucas,* Barcelona, 1968, pp. 61-72.

[7] Ibid., 62.

PART FOUR

Chapter 10

[1] Schelkle, *María, Madre del Redentor,* p. 29.

[2] Ibid., p. 34.

[3] Some of the ideas expressed here are taken from *Madre y Esposa del Verbo,* Bilbao, 1955.

[4] Schelke, *María, Madre del Redentor,* p. 44.

[5] On the historical value of the Virgin Birth, see Schelkle, *María, Madre del Redentor,* pp. 43-70.

[6] Ibid., p. 69.

[7] Ibid., p. 70.

[8] Gechter, *María en el Evangelio,* pp. 190-191.

Chapter 11

[9] Ibid., p. 284.

Chapter 12

[10] Ibid., p. 349.
[11] Ibid., p. 351.

Chapter 13

[12] R. Laurentin, *La Cuestión Mariana*, p. 188.

Chapter 14

[13] *La Biblia y su Mensaje,* No. 61, p. 4.

auline BOOKS & MEDIA

CALIFORNIA
 3908 Sepulveda Blvd., Culver City, CA 90230; 310-397-8676
 5945 Balboa Ave., San Diego, CA 92111; 619-565-9181
 46 Geary Street, San Francisco, CA 94108; 415-781-5180

FLORIDA
 145 S.W. 107th Ave., Miami, FL 33174; 305-559-6715

HAWAII
 1143 Bishop Street, Honolulu, HI 96813; 808-521-2731

ILLINOIS
 172 North Michigan Ave., Chicago, IL 60601; 312-346-4228

LOUISIANA
 4403 Veterans Memorial Blvd., Metairie, LA 70006; 504-887-7631

MASSACHUSETTS
 50 St. Paul's Ave., Jamaica Plain, Boston, MA 02130; 617-522-8911
 Rte. 1, 885 Providence Hwy., Dedham, MA 02026; 617-326-5385

MISSOURI
 9804 Watson Rd., St. Louis, MO 63126; 314-965-3512

NEW JERSEY
 561 U.S. Route 1, Wick Plaza, Edison, NJ 08817; 732-572-1200

NEW YORK
 150 East 52nd Street, New York, NY 10022; 212-754-1110
 78 Fort Place, Staten Island, NY 10301; 718-447-5071

OHIO
 2105 Ontario Street, Cleveland, OH 44115; 216-621-9427

PENNSYLVANIA
 9171-A Roosevelt Blvd., Philadelphia, PA 19114; 215-676-9494

SOUTH CAROLINA
 243 King Street, Charleston, SC 29401; 803-577-0175

TENNESSEE
 4811 Poplar Ave., Memphis, TN 38117; 901-761-2987

TEXAS
 114 Main Plaza, San Antonio, TX 78205; 210-224-8101

VIRGINIA
 1025 King Street, Alexandria, VA 22314; 703-549-3806

CANADA
 3022 Dufferin Street, Toronto, Ontario, Canada M6B 3T5; 416-781-9131
 1155 Yonge Street, Toronto, Ontario, Canada M4T 1W2; 416-934-3440